Best wishes!
Charles Stinson
Psalm 92:12-14

Hogtown

ALSO BY CHARLES STINSON

ALEXANDER
The Servant Boy Who Became a Colonial Virginia Frontiersman

Published by
INFINITY PUBLISHING 2007

Available at:

www.buybooksontheweb.com
Amazon.com
Borders.com
Barnes & Nobles.com
or
Toll-free (877) BUY-BOOK

© 2008 by Charles Stinson
All rights reserved. Published 2008

ISBN: 978-0-9779523-1-1

Printed in the United States of America
Published by Blackwell Press, Lynchburg, Virginia

Contact Blackwell Press at:
311 Rivermont Avenue
Lynchburg, Virginia 24504
434-528-4665
Email: Sales @LynchsFerry.com
www.LynchsFerry.com

Table of Contents

PART ONE:
Hogtown,
Its Origin and Scorn

Chapter 1 Welcome to Madison Heights 3
Chapter 2 Why do people call it Hogtown? 9
Chapter 3 Yeah, I'm from Hogtown! So what? 15

PART TWO:
Living in Hogtown

Chapter 4 I need a job…close by 25
Chapter 5 Where's the best place to shop? 37
Chapter 6 Attending School 47
Chapter 7 In Case of Emergency 59

PART THREE:
People, Places,
and Animals

Chapter 8 John Mayberry and the monkey 67
Chapter 9 Bill Layne and his dog Bruce 73
Chapter 10 Plowmen and their Horses 79
Chapter 11 Samuel E. "Sam" Tyree, the antagonist 83
Chapter 12 Edwin E. "Buzzy" McBride, the paperboy . 87
Chapter 13 James R. "Jimmie" Turner, the gutsy one .. 89
Chapter 14 Jimmie Ray, the photographer 91
Chapter 15 Raymond Deal, the sand man 103
Chapter 16 Willie "Sweetie" Hughes, the river man .. 109
Chapter 17 Clayton Wright, the indescribable one ... 113
Chapter 18 Harry Walton, the barber 119
Chapter 19 John Holley, Jr. and a World War II story. 123
Chapter 20 Movers and Shakers 125
Chapter 21 The last of the peddlers 129
Chapter 22 "Dumpsey's" 133
Chapter 23 "The Mighty W.T." 135

PART FOUR:
My Gang

Chapter 24 Boy Scout Troop 33.................... 143
Chapter 25 Our Band........................ 149
Chapter 26 Cousins 153
Chapter 27 The rest of the gang................. 155
Chapter 28 Recreation 161

PART FIVE:
Miscellaneous

Chapter 29 The influence of the churches.......... 173
Chapter 30 Shrader Field....................... 185
Chapter 31 The old homestead 191

PART SIX:
What does the future hold?

Chapter 32 Gloom, doom, or transformation?....... 201
Chapter 33 The Madison Heights Goat 205

Acknowledgments

This book would not exist in its present form if it were not for the help I received from by my two older brothers, Earl and Ralph Stinson, born in 1926 and 1928 respectively. They have knowledge about growing up in Madison Heights that I do not have and were also able to identify people in some of the older pictures that I could not. Their contribution to this volume has been priceless and I thank them for it. I might add that they have been longsuffering as they endured my many questions and visits.

Although my mother died in 1984, I must also recognize her contribution to this book. She was a picture taker. Not only did she take pictures, but also organized them and placed them in albums. She did the same thing with her scrapbooks. As she grew older, she numbered them and decided which child should receive which volume at her death. Her insight in doing this many years ago has provided a tremendous resource for me to use.

I would also like to recognize the contribution my wife, Irene, has made. Not only did she encourage me in writing, but has also been unselfish about the many hours I have taken from other things to work on this book. Much of that time really belonged to her. In addition, she has read parts of the manuscript as I've completed them and offered her suggestions.

My two sons, Mike and Tim, have taken time from their busy schedules to respond to my calls for help with editing questions. Each of them deserves much credit for this work. Mike has also worked diligently to do a final edit for me before I send it to the publisher. His work would probably be flawless if he could keep me from making changes to the original while I am waiting. I take the blame for any uncorrected mistakes that may appear in the book.

My daughter, Becky, has used the gift of encouragement to offer her support as she watched me struggle through another manuscript for over a year. She is waiting patiently for the finished product so she can learn more about her roots and the community she moved away from when she was eleven years old.

Many pictures in this book that are credited to Jimmie Ray have been shared with me by his family members and others from the Madison Heights community. I am indebted to each of them for their willingness to share their possessions. I want to give a special thanks to Jimmie's family members Ann Baldwin, Kyle Baldwin, Debbie Woody, and Rhonda Johnson, who have encouraged me and worked untiringly to help me collect many of these pictures. Also, I am indebted to Nancy Marion of The Design Group in Lynchburg, who has given me invaluable assistance with the negatives and prints and worked with the family members to preserve the photographic treasure that Jimmie Ray left behind. Because of the kindness of these people, a written and visual record of this outstanding photographer will be established for the generations who follow us. I have tried diligently to accurately identify as many people as I could in the pictures and receive permission to use them where appropriate. Obviously, this isn't always possible, especially with group pictures. I apologize for any mistakes I have made.

Finally, I would like to offer my thanks to everyone who has encouraged me and offered their assistance, they are too numerous to mention by name. Interest in this project has been unbelievable. Not only have I received a great deal of information, but I have learned there is a tremendous desire to record and preserve the history of Madison Heights as it has played out in so many people's lives. I give thanks to God for any good thing that comes from our combined efforts to reach this goal.

Dedication

HERMAN AND VIOLA STINSON
50th wedding anniversary, 1970

It is with humility that I dedicate this book to my parents, Herman David Stinson (1892-1987) and Lelia Viola Marks Stinson (1903-1984). Not only did they give life to seven children in Madison Heights, but also gave us a home where we found acceptance, love, and stability. Our friends were always welcome and many found a family environment at our house they had never experienced anywhere else. Although mama and daddy were strong disciplinarians, they loved and encouraged every child that entered their doors. We were blessed to have such parents.

Christmas 1951

This was the last Christmas my parents enjoyed the blessing of having all seven of their children alive. On December 2, 1952, my oldest brother, Frank Owen Stinson, 31, was injured in an automobile accident and died December 21st. He was buried two days later. Christmas, which we had always loved and celebrated as a family, was almost unbearable that year. Although we continued our annual Christmas celebrations they were never the same.

Introduction

"What're you Hogtown boys doing in town this time of night?" asked the loud man as he walked into the Texas Tavern and seated himself on the only empty stool at the counter.

"Been to a stage show at the Isis," said one of the boys, as he glanced at the man, "stayed to see it twice."

"Who'd you see?"

"Grandpa Jones."

Texas Tavern 1935-1969

The other two boys never acknowledged the man's presence as they continued eating their hot dogs, but they were aware of the probing glances from the other customers in response to the Hogtown remark. Finishing their food, the three stood to leave.

"The buses stopped running at ten," said the man, "how you gonna get home?"

"Walk."

"Wait 'til I eat and you can ride with me."

The boys started to sit back down, but one of the countermen said, "You boys wait outside if you're through eating. Leave those seats open for customers."

Making no comment, the three moved outside to the sidewalk to wait for their ride home.

Hogtown. Everybody in the area knew where it was. As the James River winds its way through central Virginia, it forms the northern boundary for the city of Lynchburg. Williams Viaduct was the only bridge across the river into Lynchburg from 1919 until 1954. Single lane traffic moved in both directions on the bridge and

WILLIAMS VIADUCT
A wreck at the northern end of the bridge, probably another runaway truck coming downhill. This was a frequent occurrence on the steep hill

a sidewalk on the west side provided a safe haven for walkers until a southbound bus or tractor trailer crowded into part of their space. When you crossed the bridge from Lynchburg into Amherst County, you were in the community of Madison Heights, disparagingly called Hogtown by many Lynchburg residents.

Madison Heights residents often referred to themselves and each other as being from Hogtown in a playful, good-spirited way. The name was even used as a sort of badge of honor by some of its residents when referring to each other and their community because they were generally proud of who they were. It was a different story when the word was cast at them by an outsider and was often considered sufficient reason for a fight or at least a strong verbal response.

What was the origin of this name and why did it evoke such hostile feelings from Madison Heights residents? One of my reasons for writing this book is to attempt to answer these two questions. Obviously, residents from past generations could have

A view towards Madison Heights from Lynchburg

answered them more easily, but they left few written records on the subject. They are dead, but the Hogtown name that existed in their day lives on.

When I started searching for answers, I began with my two older brothers, Earl and Ralph. I wanted to know what they thought the origin of the Hogtown name might be and also hear some of their stories. Our parents married in 1920, lived in Madison Heights their entire married life, and raised seven children there. Earl, Ralph, and I are the only remaining members of that family.

Another reason for this book is to share my story and leave a written record about what it was like to grow up in Madison Heights, Virginia during the middle of the Twentieth Century. Sixty years ago, a journey across the bridge in the previous picture would have taken you to my hometown. I invite you to journey back in time with me and cross that bridge today. I'll introduce you to my family and some of my friends and take you on a tour of Hogtown. While we're traveling around you can listen to some of the stories about what life was like there in the last century. Come on. Let's get started.

Charles Stinson
Forest, Virginia
2008

PART ONE:

*Hogtown,
Its Origin and Scorn*

CHAPTER 1

Welcome to Madison Heights

How do you define the boundaries of such an ambiguous area as Madison Heights? Some would probably answer, "It depends on who you ask." On the preceding pages it was noted that the James River formed the southern boundary, but what about the rest of the community?

In recent years a new phrase, "Old Town Madison Heights," has developed in an attempt to define this area. It even has an "Old Town Connector" road. It is an appropriate name and helps describe the neighborhood that I grew up in. Other Virginia towns like Fredricksburg, Yorktown, and Williamsburg use the "Old Town" designation to define a restored historic area worthy of a visit. This is not the situation in Madison Heights; there it is used to define a locality that has been neglected and is deteriorating.

In all fairness to the current residents, they are not all guilty of the above charges. Many of them are second-and third-generation inhabitants who take pride in their property. Even with these exceptions, Old Town Madison Heights is dangerously close to extinction. If it survives, intervention needs to be made quickly on its behalf.

Let me return to the initial question about defining its boundaries. A current map of the area will provide us with a simple answer. The triangle formed by the James River, The Lynchburg Expressway on the East, and Business 29 on the West would encompass Madison Heights as it originally existed and remained for many years.

I will make three exceptions to the above paragraph. First, I would extend the northern boundary several blocks to include Phelps Road, the location of Madison Heights High School and Elementary School. Secondly, the area would have been much smaller before the construction of Business 29. Prior to that, the western boundary would have been Lynch's Ferry Road and northern Main Street. This route was constructed in the early 1800s as part of the Stage Road from Charlottesville to Lynchburg.

When I was a child, most locals called Business 29 "the new road." Lynch's Ferry Road was called "the old road" because it had served as the main road through Madison Heights for over a century. Many older residents still refer to the hill rising up from the end of the John Lynch Bridge as the "new road hill."

The final exception would be to acknowledge that some people who lived slightly outside this triangle considered themselves Madison Heights residents. I do not to mean to imply they were not.

In my early years I might have said, "Madison Heights stops at the end of the sidewalk." A sidewalk began at the southern end of Main Street and ended a mile away at the schools on Phelps Road. Generally speaking, the school children walked it twice a day unless they had a nickel to ride the bus (more about that later). The sidewalk is one of the few things in Madison Heights that has experienced little change except it was later extended beyond the schools. Charles Irvin, a senior citizen from the community, writes in *Amherst County Virginia Heritage Vol. II* (Walsworth Publishing Co. 2004) that "the sidewalks, rock walls, and a sewer line" were built during the Great Depression of the late 1930s by the Civilian Conservation Corps (CCC).

Walking to school

The above paragraph is not meant to imply that those who lived north of the schools were not considered part of The Madison Heights community. They were simply not part of the Old Town. Interestingly enough, after the expressway was built in 1954, much of the development that occurred north of its intersection with Business 29 was the result of Old Town residents moving into that area. Lyttleton Lane, Ridge Street, Mays Street, and Seminole Drive were among those places developed during that era.

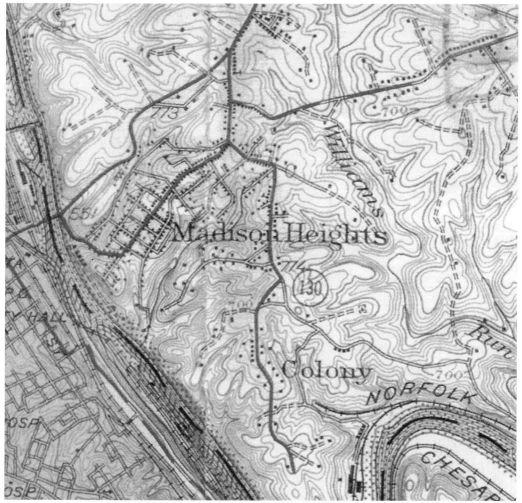

1944 map of Madison Heights

Colony Road and Wright Shop Road were important connectors to residential areas. As the name implies, Colony Road was the main connecting link from Main Street in Madison Heights to "The Colony," an institution that was established as an Epilepsy Colony in 1910. The facility has undergone several name changes and became known as the Central Virginia Training Center in 1983. The above picture shows the intersection of these two roads shortly after the new extension (left) to Business 29 was built. That new road is now appropriately called Old Town Connector.

Transportation to the Colony campus was a problem in the early days as seen in communications from that facility informing potential visitors *"if they lacked an automobile, they could take the jitney from Lynchburg to Madison Heights and walk the final mile to the Colony."* (For those who don't know what a "jitney" is, be patient; I'll get to that a little later also). The facility made it clear that it was unable to provide transportation or lodging for visitors. It was an entity unto itself and has undergone many changes. In 1972 it housed a record 3,686 residents, but has only about 500 now.

What happened to those 3,000 plus residents that once lived at the Colony? That's an interesting question that I can only partially answer. During my years in Madison Heights I drove through the Colony campus many times. I would drive slowly because the streets were thronged with residents (we called them patients) who delighted in seeing a car and outsiders. They would call to us, wave at us, shoot at us with their toy pistols, and generally exhibit a camaraderie not found many places. They were always under the watchful eye of one of the employees or attendants as they were called.

Main Street and Colony Road

The Colony employed an Athletic Director named Mr. Files. They sponsored a softball team in the church league and so did my church, Madison Heights Baptist. They had uniforms, but we didn't. The Colony team was almost unbeatable. Those guys lived to play ball and they did it well. There was always a large turnout of patients for the games and they took great delight in removing any spot of dirt from our automobiles while the game was in progress. When we were teenagers and wanted to play ball in the summer we would call Mr. Files and ask if they wanted to play a game. If they did, he would tell us what time and we would walk over and play them. We always lost.

The Colony had a huge farm operation that had been started in the earliest days and continued until the 1950s. They maintained herds of Holstein dairy cattle and several breeds of hogs. They raised grain crops and hay for the livestock and vegetables for the residents. The farm, which employed many of the facility residents, usually operated for a profit and provided much of the food the residents ate for many years. By the late 1950s the farm operation was discontinued.

In 1972 the facility discontinued all but emergency admissions because of overcrowding and was ordered by the state to reduce resident population by 10% annually. By 1979 overcrowding was further reduced when the state created three additional regional centers for the mentally handicapped. Other factors such as the creation of community service boards and the establishment of discharge planning as part of the admissions procedure served to further reduce the population.

The exodus started to reduce the population and thousands of mentally challenged men and women were sent out (some say dumped) into new social settings that they had never experienced before. After the exodus, I would often see some of them walking around Lynchburg holding hands like little lost children. Others were scattered throughout the state to group homes in other communities. Many of them had been moved from the only home they had ever known. I have heard stories that some of them ended up in high-dollar psychiatric care hospitals for temporary help from their inability to cope with their new freedom. These were sometimes brought in by police restrained in handcuffs. One can only wonder about the abuse some of them must have suffered in their new and less protected environment.

In March 2008 I rode through the Colony campus for the first time in years. I never saw a resident. I only saw a few employees as they walked from one building to another. What I did see were the big residential buildings that are sitting empty and deteriorating. Two days later I read in the local paper that Virginia is suffering from a shortage of beds to meet the needs of the mentally ill. Something is wrong with this picture.

The post office at Colony, Virginia

Beyond the Colony, but accessible only through Colony grounds, was the little community called VC or Vee Cee, which was an abbreviation for Virginia-Carolina, a fertilizer-producing plant located near the railroad and the James River. It is shown on the preceding map. A few employee houses were located near the plant and five other houses for management were located high on the hill above the plant. These houses were accessible by a road through the Colony campus or by a long flight of wooden steps from the plant. These steps were not for the fainthearted! Neither the Colony nor "The Fertilizer" (as it was called) was considered part of the old Madison Heights community.

My family was friends with the Casey family who lived in one of the management houses for the Fertilizer. I remember visiting them during the 1940s. The plant superintendent lived next door. The occupant of that position apparently changed frequently because I remember several men who served in that capacity. When Mr.

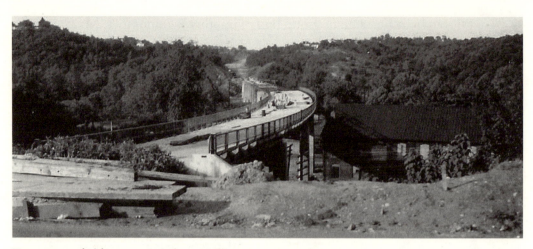

Expressway bridge construction, 1954

Barker lived there, his daughter Joan attended school with me, but they moved before she graduated.

In 1954, Meredith G. Burnette was the superintendent. His daughter, Mary Jane, graduated from Madison Heights High School and married my cousin Massie "Petey" Stinson. She remembers her dad going to Lynchburg to the bank each Friday and receiving the plant payroll in cash. The bank suggested that he place the money in a brown paper lunch bag for security reasons. It would appear he was carrying his lunch and not money. If a cash payroll seems strange to us today, we need to remember that there were no banks in Madison Heights, transportation was limited, and checks were difficult to cash. The Fertilizer closed around 1965.

Wright Shop Road began at Main Street beside Oscar Bryant's Store. It immediately started a long downhill journey to William's Run, a creek at the bottom of the hill, and continued up an even steeper hill on the other side. Madison Heights residents often referred to that stretch of road as "Creek Hill," a name that was often used interchangeably with Wright Shop Road. The people who lived beyond the creek would generally not be considered part of the Old Town of Madison Heights. The entrance to Wright Shop Road was relocated when the Expressway was constructed in 1954, and again when the new bypass was built in 2005.

Chapter 2

Why Do People Call it Hogtown?

I decided to call Ralph first and see what his answer was to the above question. After exchanging some small talk, I said, "I have a question for you."

"Let me hear it."

"Why do people call Madison Heights Hogtown?"

"Because the people used to raise a lot of hogs, I guess."

"People raised hogs everywhere. Do you think they raised more in Madison Heights than other places?"

"I wouldn't think so, but when we were growing up most families raised one or two hogs for food."

"Did you ever hear of anyone in Madison Heights raising hogs on a large scale except Tommy Riner and his daddy?"

"No. Mr. Jesse Tyree raised a few to sell after he retired, but not many. I don't know of any others."

There appear to be at least three schools of thought on the origin of the name and all of them seem to have some merit. The first is the one that Ralph and I assumed was correct. We thought people called our community Hogtown simply because in the old days, a lot of the folks who lived there raised hogs.

While many families did raise one or two hogs each year for meat, that was a common practice in America until the middle of the twentieth century. My brother-in-law, Tommy Riner, and his father, William, raised a large number of hogs each year

Ralph Stinson, "The Goldfish Man"

to sell. They lived on what is now Seminole Drive, only a short distance from Route 29. They continued hog farming until the early 1950s. I am not aware of any other hog production in Madison Heights at any time on a scale that would have justified our community being called Hogtown.

My dad, like most of our neighbors, usually raised one or two hogs each year to help feed his large family. This was not an uncommon practice and also continued into the early 1950s. Mr. Marvin "Pomp" Bryant, who lived on the corner of Fourth and Clark Streets, was the official hog killer during the 1940s. Some of the families who raised hogs would get enough help to herd them through the streets to Mr. Bryant's where they would be killed, semi-processed, and delivered back to the owners. Even though he was very young, Alfred Bryant says he remembers seeing the pigs herded down the street to his grandfather's house. Other owners chose to kill their hogs at their own homes. Three major requirements for "hog-killing day" were cold weather, a scalding trough, and lots of manpower. Again, this practice was still common in many places until the last half of the twentieth century and hardly seems sufficient cause for naming our community Hogtown. I concluded there must be another reason.

Jesse and Cora Tyree and their hogs 1945

A second possible reason was listed in a series of articles published in March 2006 in the Amherst County newspaper, *New Era Progress*. Reporter Aaron Lee and Managing Editor David Hylton spent over two months visiting old town Madison Heights and interviewing some of its senior residents who have lived their entire lives in the community. One of the things they discovered was that the Confederate Army Engineering Department had also labeled the community "Scuffletown." One definition that Webster gives for scuffle is *"to struggle (as by working odd jobs) to get by."* To me, that name suggests a community of people who worked hard to provide for their families. If that was the intent of the name, it is one to be proud of and not one to be used scornfully. Madison Heights has always been known as a "blue collar" community of Lynchburg. Although the name "Scuffletown" did not survive as another name for Madison Heights, the name Hogtown still lingers on. Interestingly enough, there are several other communities in Virginia that are called "Scuffletown."

The above-mentioned articles also stated that *"Madison Heights was once a thriving market for the slaughterhouse business that earned it the infamous nickname Hogtown."* I questioned the accuracy of that view since I can only verify one slaughterhouse in Madison Heights. It was Shaner's Slaughterhouse on "The Old Road" (now Lynch's Ferry Road).

Mr. Charlie P. Shaner owned the slaughterhouse in Madison Heights and also a meat market on Twelfth Street in Lynchburg. He apparently was a successful businessman and lived a short distance from the slaughterhouse in a fine home. John "Dutch" Gregory and Frank Casey operated the slaughterhouse in the late 1930s and early 1940s. Although I never visited the operation I have talked to others who did. Some people were left with permanent memories from their visit that they wish they didn't have.

Although I was too young to remember, I was told that the blood from the operation was released directly into the nearby creek, which emptied into the James River. I was not surprised to learn that, since most of the creeks in the Madison Heights and Lynchburg area still carried raw sewage into the James River many years after the above dates. Mr. Shaner's grandson, George W. Abbott, said the Jewish community also used the facility one day a week for their slaughtering needs that was overseen by the Rabbi.

Around 1950 another slaughterhouse operated near Monroe called Blankenship's Slaughterhouse. I know they slaughtered cows, calves, hogs, and maybe other animals, but it did not exist just to slaughter hogs.

When the map for the *Stage Road from Charlottesville to Lynchburg* was made in 1828, the creek that was parallel to Lynch's Ferry Road was listed on the map as Tanyard Creek, indicating that a tanyard may have existed there even

George W. Abbott

Richard Earl Stinson

before the road was built. Running water was an absolute necessity for a tanyard operation. Again, these businesses, which tanned animal hides for the leather, hardly dealt with hog skin. This additional fact certainly does not provide a reason for calling the area Hogtown.

When I raised the question about the origin of the name with my brother Earl, he shared a third possible answer. It was one he had heard all his life and the one that I believe is correct. It places the origin of the name at a time much earlier than any listed above. My phone call to Earl began with the same question I had asked Ralph: "Why do people call Madison Heights Hogtown?"

"When Lynchburg passed a law that people couldn't raise hogs in the city, they started raising them across the river. At least, that's what I've always been told."

"I need to find some proof for that. I wonder what year that was?"

"I don't know, but they've been calling it Hogtown for a long time.

Eighty-four-year-old Bill Layne, a lifelong resident of Madison Heights, agreed with Earl and said that's what he had always heard. Eighty-five-year-old Dr. Bill Cook, another Madison Heights native, agreed with them. (Interestingly enough, a Bedford County resident later shared the same story with me.) This would mean that when the law was changed, Lynchburg residents would have needed to purchase or rent land in Madison Heights or contract with the residents there to raise hogs for them. Since hogs require daily care, it is reasonable to assume that this is probably what happened.

An article published in the *Virginia History Digest*, 21 October 2001, quotes Scott Smith, a historian from Lynchburg, Virginia and strongly supports this premise and offers additional proof. Smith was commenting on an old inventory he had found that listed "11 head of hogs, 2 cows and cafries, and 1 Horse." He wrote, *"I would hope that this person lived on at least 100 acres in the countryside rather than 1½ to 2 acres in town if merely for the sake of his neighbors. Interestingly enough, Lynchburg enacted an ordinance in the early 19th century (a few years after this inventory) that banned hogs from being raised within the town limits. John Lynch's other town, Madison, on the north bank of the James, did not have this ordinance, and so Madison (now Madison Heights) earned the nickname of "Hogtown."*

When Lynchburg passed this ordinance in the early 1800s forbidding its residents to raise hogs in town, the hog-raising business apparently moved across the river. Those "Scuffletown" residents (though they had not yet been called that) had an opportunity for another "odd job" to help in their "struggle to get by" and provide for their families.

Some may wonder why Lynchburg folks were so determined to raise hogs even after the new law was enacted. That really should be no surprise to anyone familiar with raising a hog for food. No other meat source existed that could be raised so quickly, preserved so inexpensively, and provide meat for such an extended time for a family. Salt and smoke would preserve hundreds of pounds of ham and bacon for a family for a year. The lard rendered from a hog would serve a kitchen for many months. Freshly ground sausage was a welcome addition to the eggs gathered from the backyard chicken house and served with fried apples and biscuits. This fare, found on many breakfast tables, was usually the same that was found in the children's lunch bags as they went off to school and dad's lunch as he went to work. Someone once commented, "they used everything about a hog except its squeal" and this is close to the truth. Although some parts of the hog that were eaten would not appeal to everyone, some parts were considered a delicacy. Those who have never eaten fresh tenderloin on "hog killing day" are truly to be pitied.

Neither is the importance of hog raising confined to the last two centuries in America. For those who are interested, a trip to the Governor's Palace at Colonial Williamsburg (built in 1710-12) will reveal a "smokehouse" in the side yard with cured hams, shoulders, and middling meat hanging inside. Although hogs were locally grown, butchered, and cured during Colonial times, a guide recently explained to me that those currently on display "were purchased from Smithfield."

It was in the late 1940s when we raised our last hogs. A Lynchburg friend and co-worker, Jimmie Walker, (who later co-founded W&W Novelty in Lynchburg) convinced daddy that they should raise two pigs. Mr. Walker would supply the pigs and feed, daddy would supply the pigpen and labor, and each would have a hog to butcher in the fall. The arrangement worked well for both of them, but not for me. As a young teenager and the last unemployed boy at home, I had to feed those pigs every day. I suppose the Lynchburg residents of the early 1800s worked out similar agreements with the Madison Heights folks. The arrangement apparently worked well for both groups, but it stigmatized our community, with the name Hogtown that is still in use today.

It would be interesting to know what kind of agreement was worked out between the Lynchburg owners and the Madison Heights caregivers to provide feed for the hogs. Normally, a household that was raising one or two pigs for themselves would feed them "slop." Every household had a "slop bucket" where the table scraps and other disposable food waste was thrown. At the end of the day, water was added to the bucket with a scoop of commercial hog food (if available). It was all stirred together, carried to the hog pen and poured into the hog trough. It may sound gross to you, but the hogs loved it. One household would have difficulty supplying enough slop for extra pigs unless food was bought.

HOG KILLING TIME
By Mrs. J. L. Benton

When I am old and have little to do
But twiddle my fingers and sip at my stew
I shall sit by the fire and try to remember
Hog Killing time in the month of December

Then all of the neighbors brought hogs nice and fat
And everyone used the same scalding vat…
How the farmers did work-as only farmers can
And in no time at all 'twas a "call for a pan."
It was turn and go-so much to do…
So much to prepare before we were through-
Chitterlings to turn, sausage to grind,
Lard to cook, paddles to find.

But mixed with it all a good joke was told-
Laughter and fellowship for young and for old.
My! The food on those tables-we ate till we hurt-
Then sliced three big pies for a whopping dessert.
But back to the work-whether rain, snow, or sleet,
We had to get busy on the ears, nose, and feet.

Such fun did we have-we and each neighbor-
Sharing our laughter and sharing our labor.
If for some reason things didn't go right,
We would stick to our jobs well into the night.
Oh, yes, we got tired-our poor muscles ached,
But our job was well done the next morn when we waked.

So I'm sure when I'm old and can't carry my load
And I'm nearing the end of life's long, busy road,
I shall sit by my fire and with pleasure remember
Hog killing time in the month of December.

THIS POEM AND PICTURE WERE ON A NEWSPAPER CLIPPING FOUND IN THE POSSESSIONS OF MY SISTER MARGARET STINSON COMPTON AFTER HER DEATH IN 2000.
ORIGIN OF THE CLIPPING IS UNKNOWN.

Chapter 3

"Yeah, I'm from Hogtown! So What?"

Continuing my Hogtown discussion with Earl and Ralph, each of us could remember many times when we felt the sting of sarcastic remarks about being "from Hogtown." Occasionally these remarks backfired. Earl's father-in-law, John Holley, Sr., who lived on Clark Street in Madison Heights, worked his entire life for the N&W railroad and was a gifted machinist. He literally could make or repair almost anything and proved it by building a scale-model train complete with a steam engine and cars large enough to ride. He named it the "B & R Railroad" the first two initials of his oldest grandchildren and ran it on a track that wound through his yard.

Earl told me the following Hogtown story about Mr. Holley that emphasized both the degrading use of the word by an outsider and the proud response of one who lived there. Mr. Holley went to Lynchburg one day to buy a new bedroom suite from a furniture store located on Main Street. Prior to his purchase, he was having lunch in one of the downtown cafes. The owner of the furniture store he had come to patronize was also having lunch there and Mr. Holley overheard him making offensive remarks about Hogtown and its people. Mr. Holley waited until the man had finished his lunch and returned to the store and then he also went there. When he entered, the same man welcomed him and asked, "What can I help you with today?"

"I came to town today to buy a bedroom suite from you," replied Mr. Holley. "But after hearing your remarks at lunch today about Hogtown and its people, I

JOHN HOLLEY AND HIS TRAIN
The engine and coal car of the B & R Railroad train he built

Test run of the Holley train

just came in here to tell you that I live in Hogtown and I'm not buying anything from you!"

Ralph and Earl both worked at J.W. Bibee's grocery store on the corner of Seventh and Main Streets in Lynchburg when they were teenagers. Ralph recalls telling people at the Lynchburg store that he lived in Madison Heights and receiving a snobbish look from them. Even if they never used the word, their looks said, "You're from Hogtown." What was it about that name that conferred a second-rate status to its residents and usually provoked them to anger?

Madison Heights Baptist Church, 50th Anniversary Celebration, June 8, 1941

Billy Sunday offering envelope

My dad was a member of Madison Heights Baptist Church from the early 1920s until his death in 1987. He served as an usher in the great Billy Sunday Crusade held in Lynchburg in 1922. I remember several stories that he told about that event. One was about a big parade that was held in downtown Lynchburg in preparation for the meetings. Churches throughout the area sent various groups to march in the parade, each carrying a banner to identify their church. My dad marched with his men's Sunday School class from Madison Heights Baptist Church. As they passed by the crowds that stood along Main Street, one of the bystanders yelled loudly, "Here comes the Hogtown Baptists!" An infuriated class member instinctively shouted a non-Christian response to the individual. He called the man a name and told him where he could go…and it wasn't to the Crusade Meetings being held at the Tobacco Warehouse. The class teacher, Mr. Montague Nicholas, quickly intervened and reminded the class member that his conduct was unacceptable and a poor testimony to others.

Why were the hard-working people of Madison Heights condemned to a second-rate status for raising hogs? This was puzzling to me at first, but has gradually become clearer. The old law of the "have's" and the "have not's" probably explains it best. The things that Lynchburg had and Madison Heights did not have were many: prominent and wealthy citizens who lived in fine homes, a local government, police and fire protection, public transportation, banks, a shopping district, hospitals, specialized doctors, and diverse industry.

These differences alone would have affected the relative social status of the residents of the two communities. With the introduction of the Lynchburg law forbidding hog raising and a willingness of the people on the other side of the river to perform this lowly service for a fee, the stage was set to widen the existing status gap between the two communities and coin the new name, "Hogtown," for Madison Heights.

One of the best-known parables of Jesus is The Parable of the Prodigal Son (Luke 15:11-32). In the story the prodigal wasted everything he had in wild living. When he had nothing left he accepted a job feeding pigs for a stranger. Most people interpret that as meaning he had sunk as low as he could get in his society. Perhaps that was the attitude of others towards Madison Heights citizens who performed this lowly task for their neighbors across the river. It's no wonder her citizens became irate because of the name-calling. It has only been in the last half-century that tensions between the two communities have lessened. What were once fighting words have evolved into a source of pride for many young adults in Madison Heights.

Eddie Gibson lives at the southern end of Clark Street and owns a race car which his son drives in the weekly races at South Boston. His bus, modified to carry his racecar, is a good example of the contemporary use of the Hogtown name by a current resident who is proud of his community.

In the old days, if a Lynchburg man met a pretty miss from Hogtown, he would have to be a brave person to venture across the river after dark for a date. It was almost certain that when he started home that night he would be hastened along his journey on the Amherst County side of the river with a barrage of rocks flying through the darkness. It was a fearful experience, especially for those traveling on foot. Many of the young men never returned to Madison Heights to see their sweetheart. Those of us who have traveled through the mountains of Virginia are familiar with

Hogtown Hauler bus

The steps at Main and Third

the warning signs that say "WATCH FOR FALLEN ROCKS." A more appropriate sign in Madison Heights during the old days would have been "WATCH FOR FLYING ROCKS."

This tradition continued into the 1950s. Third Street between Church and Main comes to a dead end before it reaches Main. Two heavy sections of fence blocked the street to prevent an automobile from plunging down a steep bank. They no longer exist, but were once located where the pickup truck is parked in the previous picture. The concrete steps provided access to the street for walkers. Local residents were amazed one morning to find the fence knocked down and tire tracks down the bank, but no car. Everyone wondered who the driver was and how it was possible for a car to survive a trip down the steep bank and continue its journey. The mystery remained unsolved for a long time until I was in a restaurant one day and overheard a young man from Lynchburg telling his friends about his first date with a Madison Heights girl. When he returned to his car, a gang of boys appeared in the street behind him and began "rocking" him and his car. He had no place to escape except forward and that's the way he went. Not easily discouraged, the young man continued dating his Hogtown girl (who happened to be one of my classmates) and eventually married her.

Rock throwing was not reserved only for the harassment of outsiders. Disagreements between children often resulted in a "rock battle" although our parents forbade them. I was deeply engaged in one near my grandmother's house one day when somebody told my Mama what was taking place. With seven children of her own to oversee plus the endless line of others that passed through our place, Mama dispensed justice quickly and firmly, often with whatever happened to be handy. On this particular day, a dog leash was in easy reach as she left her kitchen and started toward the battle zone. Unfortunately for me, I had on short pants that day. I never saw her coming up behind me, but should have been suspicious when I saw my opposition scattering. I was unaware of her presence until I felt her grip on my arm and the sting of the leather leash on my bare legs!

I suppose I was a slow learner, but more rock battles followed that one. In a recent conversation with Alfred Bryant (who was my neighbor in the pre-war years) he told me about "one of the Adcock boys" hitting him in the head with a rock during a battle in the same area mentioned above. "I saw a thousand stars," he said, "I thought he had killed me. Do you remember that?"

"No," I said. "Do you remember hitting me in the nose with a rock?"

After he finished laughing, he took an oath that he didn't remember it, but acknowledged that his uncle, Roy Riner, told him he was "the meanest kid he had ever seen." He said, "Uncle Roy said he was sitting on the front porch one day in the swing and I rode my tricycle across the porch as fast I could pedal it and ran right into his legs!"

"I believe that," I said. "You were mean. Every time we played together we would end up fighting. We had a fight at my house one day and Mama made you go home. When you reached the top of the hill, you started throwing rocks down at me. I returned the favor and crept up the path trying to offset your hilltop advantage. Just as I peeked over the crest of the hill, a rock smashed my nose." He swears he doesn't remember it, but he sure did enjoy hearing the story!

Earl once decided he was going to get rich raising Angora rabbits. After obtaining a large number of rabbits he was transferred to Lexington and I was left to provide for the bunnies. Their daily care became a despised routine for me. Ralph "Crow" Johnson was my best friend and often my shadow, spending as much time at my house as he did his. He often helped me with my chores. One evening while we were feeding the rabbits a teenage girl who lived nearby distracted him (imagine that). In a typical "boy shows off for girl" tactic, he started throwing green apples at me from a tree behind her house. Several apples painfully found their mark on my back. I warned him to stop, but as soon as I turned around to feed the rabbits he would throw an apple and then hide behind some tall weeds where I couldn't see him. I picked up a rock, dropped it into my pocket, and warned him not to hit me again.

The girl was sitting on her porch being greatly amused at my expense. When I turned back to my work he hit me in the middle of the back with a green apple. It hurt like the dickens! Enraged, I spun around and pulled the rock from my pocket. Although I couldn't see him, I knew about where he was in the weeds. I let it fly. A sickening "thump" came from the weeds and the girl on the porch gasped! I ran to the yard and found my buddy unconscious with a knot on his forehead that continued growing as I watched it. I thought he was dead, but after a short time he began to respond.

That night, there was a lawn party at the Odd Fellows Hall and we had planned to go. We loved the lawn parties. I would never have let people see me with a knot like

SHERIFF MAYLON BRYANT AT A WRECK
A wreck at the end of Williams Viaduct involving a two-ton truck driven by Bernard Bryant "Jr." in and a tractor-trailer. Harry Linthicum, a passenger in Bryant's truck, and the tractor-trailer driver were killed. Virginia State Trooper Harold Tipton, who served in Madison Heights for many years, is shown at left center. Sheriff Bryant (foreground) had a difficult time with teenagers in Old Madison Heights during part of his tenure.

that on my head, but Crow, who was less vain than I, decided to go anyway. When anyone asked him what happened to his head he said, "Charles tried to kill me."

I could tell many other rock throwing stories, but will only share one more. During warm weather, young teenagers would play a night game called "Home Sheep." It was a form of hide and seek. Two teams would alternate hiding. When you were hidden, someone would "give a signal" by yelling "Home Sheep" and the other team would begin the search. Depending on the number and age of the players, our boundaries would be one or two blocks.

We knew every hole in every fence and hedge and every good place to hide. Years later when the Sheriff's department was trying to squelch a juvenile delinquency problem in that area, Sheriff Maylon Bryant (see picture above) told me how difficult it was to catch anyone. He said, "They seem to disappear into thin air." I laughed and said, "You're wasting your time. Those boys can move from block to block and you'll never see them."

Aaron Lee, reporter for *New Era Progress*, interviewed the current Amherst County Sheriff, Jimmy Ayers, about Old Town Madison Heights in 2006. He told a story of patrolling there one night when he was a deputy and a brick came crashing through his cruiser window. "They had some tough times in the 1970s and 1980s," he said, "but things calmed down in the 1990s."

When I was a teenager, we did some mischievous things, but we were never destructive. One of the things we liked to do for entertainment was to whistle at taxis. Cabs were numerous then and very competitive. They were always anxious for a fare, especially if they had brought someone to Madison Heights and were returning to Lynchburg empty.

Lynchburg's Radio, Grey Top, Southern, and Yellow cabs all displayed their lighted signs on the roof of their vehicles. We could see them coming for blocks, but they

Lynchburg taxi in Madison Heights

couldn't see us. As soon as they passed, we would whistle. They would hit the brakes and back up to find nobody there. They would sit there a minute and continue on. We would whistle again and they would stop and back up again. They really saw it bad in late summer and early fall when there were plenty of half-rotten apples available in backyards. Then our entertainment changed from whistling at cabs to throwing rotten apples at them. We threw lots of apples, but never threw rocks at vehicles. We only threw rocks at mean dogs and people.

Now for the last rock-throwing story. One night we were playing Home Sheep. Jimmie Turner was hiding in the yard where Emma Bryant lived with her two sisters on Clark Street. The yard was overgrown with many varieties of trees and shrubs. Jimmie, who didn't scare easily, was scared out of his senses by the appearance of what he swears was a bear walking through the yard. He escaped by plunging through a huge rose bush and running for his life. There was no doubt that he saw something and he had the wounds to prove it. We decided that we would declare that yard "off limits."

A few weeks later we were playing in that area again. Everyone was told not to enter that yard. During the search phase, one of the boys came running up and declared that he had seen "that thing that Jimmie saw!" The group all grabbed rocks from the ditch and crept up the road for a closer look. There it was, hunkered down in the yard behind a big tree. Some brave (or foolish) boy let a rock fly and it found its mark with a "whump." Everybody ran down the street to the safety of a recently installed streetlight and stared up the road watching for "the bear." "There it comes!" screamed one of the boys, and everybody started running away.

"Help me," cried a voice. All of us stopped and looked back. Two figures could be seen in the darkness, one dragging the other. We rushed back up the street and found two of the other team members. One was unconscious and bleeding profusely from his head. The other was trying to justify their presence in the "off limits" sector. When "the bear" regained consciousness he was assisted home to recover, but nobody ever told who "killed the bear" with the rock. This is not a confession.

PART TWO:

Living in Hogtown

Chapter 4

I Need a Job… Close By

Few places existed in Madison Heights for permanent employment other than grocery stores and those were mostly family operated, offering only part-time employment to others. The only exception was a Bibee's store on the corner of Main Street and Colony Road. It was large enough to have multiple employees. In a 1989 *Discover Amherst County* article about Frank Murphy, the first manager, the store was noted as being the "first supermarket in the county." Several Bibee's stores were also located in Lynchburg. I suppose these locally owned stores could be considered one of Lynchburg's first chain stores if not the first.

Bill Cook, a friend of my brother Frank, was one of the first boys to work part-time at the new Bibee's Super Market. He said he "worked from 7:00 in the morning until 10:30 at night for $1.75 per day." Before that, Bill delivered *The Daily Advance* six days a week to 140 customers. The papers cost him 9 cents per customer and he received 16 cents if he collected.

Bibee's Super Market

William A. "Bill" Cook, Jr.

Helen Whitmore, long-time clerk at Madison Square Market

Virginia Campbell and Bessie Ray hand pumping kerosene at H.M. Ray's store

Bill and Frank were in the Boy Scouts and attended Camp Tye Brook in Nelson County for summer camp in 1937 and 1938. He recalls that camp cost $1 a day. Bill graduated from Madison Heights High school in 1939. He attended medical school and after graduating returned to Lynchburg to establish his practice. My mother was as proud of Bill as she would have been of one of her own children. My brothers, Frank and Earl, also worked at the Bibee's store. After Bibee's closed their Madison Heights store, it was operated as Hollingsworth's Store and later Langford Walton and Ed Childress operated it for many years as Madison Square Market. On my one-mile walk to school each day, I would pass the Square Market as well as seven smaller stores along the sidewalk. You could purchase most anything you needed from them. Three of them sold gasoline and most of them sold kerosene, a much-needed commodity in those days. Several of them offered delivery service and credit. Before I describe other work places perhaps I should comment more about these stores that existed on Main Street in my day. (There had been other stores before my time that no longer existed, and some changed ownership or closed while I lived there.) In lower Madison Heights, where I lived on Second Street, there were three stores within easy walking distance. Wright's Store was the closest and was located on the corner of Fourth and Main. Aubrey Wright, who had assumed ownership from his father, Jim Wright, operated it. The red brick building still

Will Morris, Jim Wright, Aubrey Wright

H.M. Ray's Store

Howard And Bessie Ray, Ray's Store 1949

stands, but has been used for other purposes since the store closed. (See Chapter 17 for more details) The following picture shows three men who once operated stores on Main Street.

Bernard Bryant operated a store midway between Fifth and Sixth Streets and his son, Bernard Jr., operated it after him. The store was located beside the Post Office.

Howard and Bessie Ray operated a store at 519 Main Street. I had an interesting experience at their store shortly after the end of World War II. During the war, many things were rationed, including sugar. Because of the sugar shortage we couldn't buy bubble gum or chewing gum for a long time. Slowly, these items became available after the war ended. When news spread that some stores had bubble gum, I would stop by each store as I walked from school and ask, "You have any bubble gum?"

One day, to my surprise, Mrs. Ray said, "Yes, but you can only buy two pieces. I want the other children to be able to have some too." I bought my two pieces and hurried on, spreading the good news to every kid I met. The Double Bubble gum was scored in the center so it was easy to break in half. I broke off half and chewed and chewed. When the flavor was gone, I kept on chewing. When suppertime came, I parked it in a safe place and resumed chewing after I ate. When bedtime came, I parked it for the night on the bedpost and resumed chewing it the next day. This went on for two days before Mama caught a glimpse of the discolored gum.

"Throw that stuff away," she demanded.

"I've only been chewing it two days," I moaned.

"Throw it away now!"

It almost broke my heart as I tossed it in the coalscuttle. Many years later there was a country music song titled *"Does Your Chewing Gum Lose Its Flavor On The Bedpost Overnight?"* I think Lonzo and Oscar or one of the other country comics sang it to be funny, but it probably struck a familiar chord with many people besides me.

When I returned to school the next day I still had one piece of bubble gum. Some of the kids hadn't been able to get any and they were all trying to beg or buy from those who did. One boy, whose dad had just returned from the war, approached me and asked if I had any bubble gum.

"One piece," I answered.

"Want to sell it."

"Nope."

"I'll trade you this German medal for it," he said, reaching into his pocket to withdraw a gray medal about the size of a silver dollar. "My daddy got it off a German soldier."

I reached out and took it in my hand and studied it. A swastika was stamped on the front of it and writing was on the back. I remembered how many times I had drawn pictures of swastikas during the war and how hard it had been to get the legs all pointed the right way. My heart was pounding. I wanted that medal, but I couldn't stand the thought of parting with my last piece of bubble gum, especially since I didn't know when I would get any more.

"I'll give you half a piece for it," I said.

"Nope. I'll trade with somebody else."

"Nobody else has any left," I said with authority.

"You sure?"

"Yep."

"Give me the half a piece."

I felt really guilty about taking the medal. I expected to hear from his parents, but I never did. I still have the medal, it is the Eastern Front Medal 1941-42, and has an interesting history. It was awarded to those who had participated in the Nazi invasion

The Eastern Front Medal 1941–42

MALCOLM "BOOTS" McFADEN
Hawkins Store and Shoe Repair, later owned by "Boots" McFaden

Eisenhower at Union Station
September 26, 1952

of Russia. The cold winter of 1941-42 took a greater toll on the Germans than the Russian army and caused them to withdraw. The Germans soldiers sarcastically called it The Frozen Meat Medal.

"Up the road," as we often referred to the upper end of Main Street beyond the Post Office, Leroy and Hilda Hawkins operated the next store. Its first location was at the intersection of Main Street and the Old Road (Lynch's Ferry Road). Later it moved a block down the street to Walker's Store that was being operated by Mrs. Hawkins' aged parents, John and Matt Walker. Mrs. Walker had been the primary storekeeper while her husband operated an automobile repair shop on The Old Road. Later, Malcolm "Boots" McFaden operated an automobile body repair shop in the Hawkins store building. Leroy also operated a shoe repair shop next door to the store. His children learned the trade from him and passed it on to their children who still practice it in Lynchburg at the Cobblers Shop located in The Plaza. As already noted, the Bibee's store was at the intersection of Main and Colony Road. Not only did it provide employment for two of my brothers, Frank and Earl, but also provided a job for Ralph and me when it became Madison Square Market. I began working there afternoons and Saturdays when I was in high school. All four of us worked in the meat market. Unlike the pre-packaged meats today, everything there

Bobby Bryant, Bryant's Cash Store

was prepared to order. One afternoon, my boss, Ed Childress, came in and announced that he was going to the train station to see General Dwight Eisenhower who was campaigning for president and was making a stop in Lynchburg. He was elated when he returned and told us what "Ike" had said to the large crowd who had assembled at Union Station on Jefferson Street. "Ike said, 'They told me there wouldn't be enough people here to form a corporal's guard. This is the largest corporal's guard I have ever seen!'"

As I continued my walk to school, I would pass three more stores after I crossed Colony Road. I've already mentioned Oscar Bryant's Store at the corner of Wright Shop Road (now Campbell Street). Bobby Bryant assumed operation of this store from his father just as the Wright family and the other Bryant family had. He operated it from about 1960 to 1984. At the intersection of Main Street and Route 29, Raymond Woody operated a store and restaurant with gas pumps. A common name for such a facility in those

Woody's Filling Station

days was a "filling station." As the signs advertised he served plate lunches, Bar-B-Q-Plates (there was a barbeque pit outside) and more. A "Tourist Home" was close by to accommodate travelers. Shortly after I started to school (1941-42) there was an explosion that damaged the building extensively. When Mr. Woody rebuilt it he imbedded much of the broken colored glass into the stucco exterior where it can still be seen. The modified building still stands, but has not served as a store for many years. Frank Murphy, Sr., operated the last store along the sidewalk before I arrived at school. With eight stores along our pathway it was nearly impossible to leave home with a nickel in your pocket and return with it in the afternoon! And a greater problem was acquiring a nickel. If you couldn't get a nickel, a penny would do, since almost every store had a candy case filled with penny candy. The four-foot tall cases had solid glass fronts on them and the glass was usually smeared with fingerprints and nose prints. Mary Janes were two for a penny and so were Mint Juleps. BB Bats, Bolster Bars, chocolate drops, and other candies were also a penny. A soft drink was a nickel until I was a teenager, but I hardly ever had a nickel. All eight of these store buildings still stand, but none of them operate as a store today.

In addition to the eight grocery stores in the community, there was also one drug store called Madison Pharmacy. It was located at the intersection of Business 29 and Main Street, across from Raymond Woody's store. Tom Banton, a local druggist, built and operated the new drug store. He also built a new home next door. Tom had operated a drug store at 519 Main Street in Madison Heights next door to his home place. When he built the new drug store, H.M. Ray opened a grocery store in the building he vacated.

Madison Pharmacy

Madison Pharmacy, left to right: Helen and Jesse Whitmore, Dr. Hollingsworth, Tom Banton

The new drug store had an apartment overhead and a doctor's office beside it. After World War II, Dr. Oscar Ramsey opened his medical practice there and continued until his retirement. Dr. George Harris and Dr. Ramsey both served many years as our community doctors. Dr. John Saunders and Dr. Hollingsworth served shorter terms during the interim years. The drug store provided delivery service by bicycle. This was a nice job for some strong young boy with the fortitude of a Pony Express Rider who was never deterred by the weather. The riders didn't have to contend with Indians along the route, only mean dogs that got their exercise by chasing bikes and nipping at the ankles of the riders. If you've never had a dog's fang implanted into that sparsely covered area over your anklebone, be thankful. Richard "Dick" Nicholas was the drug store delivery boy for many years while attending high school. I never remember the store having any problem finding delivery boys because jobs were scarce. So far in this chapter I have only dealt with the stores as places of employment, and none of them were major employers. The one large employer in our area was "The Colony." Some of the people from our community worked there, but not as many as you might suppose. Most of them had automobiles, but some walked to work. Others who had no car would arrange transportation with those who did. Charlie T. Phelps lived on Warwick Street behind the Baptist Church and worked at the Colony for over 30 years as a shift supervisor in the power plant. He walked to work daily for most of these years leaving home at 5:45 each morning. He bought his first car about

Bill Layne and his car

1949, a green 1941 Chevrolet. His son Calvin says the family called it "The Green Hornet."

The majority of the adults in our community worked in Lynchburg. Some of the largest employers were "The Foundry" (Lynchburg Foundry), "The Paper Mill" (Meade Corp.), "The Shoe Factory" (multiple locations of Craddock-Terry), "Glamorgan", (Glamorgan Pipe and Foundry), and "The Hosiery Mill" (Lynchburg Hosiery Mills). There were other places that employed large number of employees, but these were some of the major ones.

W.C. "Bill" Layne lived on Stumps Hill and worked at Lynchburg Foundry for 33 years. He never owned a car until he was 78 years old, so he walked to work each morning, leaving home at four o'clock. He operated the overhead "charging crane" used to load iron ore, coke, and scrap iron into the cupola for melting. The molten iron had to be ready for pouring by seven o'clock. In his later years before retirement, he would ride a taxi to work. Once when the streets were covered with ice, the taxi couldn't get up Stumps Hill so he started walking down. He fell and slid all the way down the long hill. He laughs about it now, but remembers that his clothes were soaking wet when he reached the bottom. As this book is being written (2007), Bill is still living an active life at age 84 and also enjoying his car!

Another place where people worked was "The Railroad." In our community this usually meant the N & W railroad yard located on "The Island" (Percival's Island). Although some of my neighbors worked for The Southern Railroad, they were in the minority. When I was a child, some of the older men still went to work on "The Island" by walking a path from the end of Clark Street to the James River where they kept boats at "The Boat Landing" and then poling a boat across the river. Mr. W.W. "Walker" Freeman was one of these men. I remember when he bought his first automobile, a new 1955 Plymouth. He commented that he thought, "It would run just as fast backwards as it would forward." Perhaps his observation was based on his years as an engineer on the railroad. I think he was retired when he bought the car. During his working years he used a boat to go to and from work. His son, Walker Freeman, Jr., followed in his dad's footsteps and also became an engineer for the N&W. In a conversation with him when he was well past retirement age, he was able to tell me in great detail how the boats were built.

What's left of the boat landing

Sunday afternoon visitors 1930

Elmer Mayberry, Tom Carroll, and Marvin Tyree were other neighbors who rode the boats to work. My brother Ralph remembers helping Elmer Mayberry carry a newly built boat to the river. Mr. Mayberry recruited all the boys in the neighborhood to pick it up and carry it. No easy task, but a necessary one. Most of the route was just a footpath and would have been well over one-half of a mile.

Tom Carroll was a kind gentleman and befriended us kids. He would usually stop and talk to us each day as he walked from the boat landing to his home on Third and Main. If we had broken toys, he would often take them to work and mend them. My cousin Petey Stinson had a little double barrel shotgun made out of metal. It was spring loaded, shot corks, and you bent it open to cock it. One day it broke. When Mr. Carroll came by from work Petey showed it to him and asked him if he could fix it. He said, "Tonight before you go to bed, hide it under that little foot bridge there and I'll get it in the morning." The next day, the gun was gone. When Mr. Carroll returned that afternoon he had the gun in his hand. He had bronze welded it and it was as good as new. We were all amazed.

Other men had used the boats, but when I came along many of the older ones were gone and only two boats were left at the boat landing. In earlier years there had been more boats and two boat landings. The last one in use was referred to as "the boat landing" and the other one, a short distance downriver, was called "the old boat landing." These sites had provided destinations for people to walk to for fishing, swimming, or for a family picnic when the weather was nice. But for the men working on the island, crossing the river was never a picnic. High water and cold weather presented additional problems. Walker Freeman, Jr. told me a story about his dad falling from a boat in cold weather. He couldn't swim and was clad in heavy clothing, but was able to cling to the side of the boat until he could pull himself back inside. He almost froze before he walked to the nearby home of Sam Tyree where he could get warm by the stove. The boat landing, and nearby Magazine Hollow where

MAMIE MAYBERRY FREEMAN

Elmer Mayberry

the foundation of an old powder magazine is located, were favorite places to visit on Sunday afternoons. Dating couples often had their pictures made at these sites, especially in the boats. These homemade riverboats were plentiful along the river when I was a child. Several years ago I tried to find one and couldn't. How sad there are none left.

This undated picture of Elmer Mayberry was taken at the boat landing. With his lunch bucket in hand, he is preparing to cross the river to go to work. The boat in the background was one of the boats used by the N & W workers and probably belonged to him.

Chapter 5

Where's the Best Place to Shop?

Except for groceries and gasoline, most Madison Heights residents shopped in downtown Lynchburg. Most of the shops were on Main Street, but some were also located on Commerce and Church Streets and the connecting streets from Fifth to Thirteenth. Clothing, groceries, furniture, auto tires and parts, cameras, hunting and fishing supplies and even new automobiles could be purchased there.

Three automobile dealers were located downtown when I was a boy. Aubrey Thomas was the earliest Oldsmobile dealer I remember and John P. Hughes was the Dodge dealer. Both of these were on Commerce Street. Cary Chevrolet was on Main Street between Fifth and Sixth. All have relocated and only John P. Hughes has maintained the same name.

If you needed building supplies, you could find them at H.E. Dewitt on Commerce Street. Dabney Foundry and Machine Shop, Price and Clements Machine Shop, Abbitt Brother's Auto Repair, Harris Woodson Candy Company, printing companies, shoe factories, two flour mills, an ice company, plumbing supplies, hardware dealers, paint suppliers, Trailways and Greyhound bus terminals, and numerous banks were all conveniently located a short walk from the bus line. If for some reason you needed to travel further, the Lynchburg bus service would meet your needs.

WARNER THEATRE
I do not have the date that this picture was taken but the automobiles in the picture are late 1950s and early 1960s. Lynchburg had already changed to one-way traffic on the downtown streets when this picture was made. The movie listed on the marquee reads as follows:

Richard Burton's "Hamlet"
Mat at 2pm
Eve at 8pm

There were four movie theatres on Main Street. Most people today are familiar with the old Academy Theatre between Fifth and Sixth Street, which is being restored. The other three theatre buildings no longer remain. The Paramount stood almost directly across from the Academy and the Isis stood on the same side of Main Street between Sixth and Seventh Street. The fourth one, the Trenton, was five blocks down

Isis Theatre, June 22, 1920

the street on the corner of Main and Eleventh. It later became the Warner Theatre before it closed.

Theatres were not the only form of entertainment downtown. Two bowling alleys, one near the Academy and another next to the Trenton, provided amusement for those who enjoyed that sport. They also provided another opportunity for boys to pick up a few dollars each week serving as "pin boys," sitting up tenpins and clearing the alley when needed. They usually worked for tips only, so they really hustled to keep the game going smoothly. Like the drug store delivery boy mentioned in an earlier chapter, there were always guys standing in the wings if a job came open. Alas! Automatic pinsetters came along and another work opportunity disappeared.

For those who liked fine dining, that could also be found on Main Street. I can remember the names of three of the restaurants, White House Cafe, Town Talk and Mack and Ann. Since I never ate at any of them, I cannot comment on them except to say that when I was a boy, watching the live crabs in the window of one of them

Red Crown Bowling Alley

always fascinated me!

Those who leaned more towards inexpensive fare could find numerous lunchrooms along the sidewalks. They were sometimes referred to as "holes in the wall" because they were built in the space between two larger buildings. Most of these had a grill down one wall with a narrow workspace, a counter with stools, and a small aisle against the other wall. Of these, the Texas Tavern was in a class all by itself and has often been the subject of stories in local publications like *Lynch's Ferry*, Spring/Summer, 1997, and again in the Fall/Winter, 2007 issue. Phil's Smoke Shop was also an exception. It was located on Main Street across from the Hotel Carroll. As the name implied, they stocked a wide variety of tobacco products. In addition, they sold hamburgers and beer. Their hamburgers were among the best available.

Kresge's, Neisner Brothers, and Woolworth's were all found downtown. They were sometimes called "dime stores," "dollar stores," or "five and dime's." They had miscellaneous items for sale, even goldfish. Most of them had "lunch counters," but my favorite place was the "candy counter." Wow! You name it and it was there…and always fresh. Large bins of candy, priced by the pound. Kresge's had a large U-shaped counter with more candy than I had ever seen. You chose your candy, they would

Raylass Store

Inside Raylass Store, 1941

Reynolds Drug Store

weigh it, place it in a little white bag and you were ready to go. (And back then there was no sales tax.) I remember one year at Christmas, they had large stuffed dates rolled in white sugar. They were out of my price range so I never ate one, but I gazed at them with lust every time I passed by. Apparently they weren't as large as they seemed because I've never seen any that big since.

Raylass Department Store was located at 1005 Main Street and was different from the other stores. The 1941 picture at left is interesting because there are still cobblestones located on Main Street in front of the store. Anyone remember when they were covered over or removed? The picture below it was taken inside the store and gives an idea of some of the materials sold. Look at those prices! In the foreground, colorfast cloth prints at 10 cents a yard, boy's shirts are 15 cents and boy's polo shirts were 25 and 39 cents each. Several drugs stores were downtown: Reynold's, Jackson's, Patterson's, and Walgreen's were all located on Main Street. Several of them had lunch counters and Reynold's had a lunch counter and also sold hand dipped ice cream. Butter pecan was my favorite until one day I bit into a tiny white worm that had met its demise after burrowing into a pecan. It wasn't the fault of the drug store because it was high-quality ice cream they had purchased from a dairy, but I've never

Old buses in Madison Heights Garage

liked butter pecan as well since.

Jackson's Cut Rate Drugs was located at 821 Main Street and was the place where we usually had our film developed. They were the only one of the Main Street drug stores that did not have a lunch counter.

Allied Pharmacy was on the street level of the Allied Arts Building on Church Street. I don't remember them having a lunch counter, but they did sell some sandwiches.

So how did we get to downtown Lynchburg? Usually on the bus, or as my Mama often called it, "the jitney" or "jitney bus." I think the last term would be grammatically the same as saying "tooth dentist" since a jitney is a bus. Several years ago I began thinking about how Mama used that word. Most people would simply say "I rode the bus" or "I caught the bus." I began to research the word "jitney" and found it was a slang word of unknown origin that means "nickel" which was the original fare for

A wrecked jitney

Bus wreck on Route 29, February 12, 1949

such buses. According to *Webster's Collegiate Dictionary*, the word originated about 1903 and the fare was still a nickel when I came along. I remember when it increased to ten cents in the 1950s. To soften the impact of the increase, they began to sell three tokens for a quarter and you could ride for a token.

A second definition of a "jitney" is *"a small bus that carries passengers over a regular route according to a flexible schedule."* A search on the Internet today will still find a few "jitneys" in operation.

The Madison Heights bus line was operated by Clyde Clements and called "The Red Bus Line." The nickel fare would carry you to any destination on the line. The routes changed during later years, but for most of my bus riding years the bus turned around at Second and Main Streets. As it came down Main Street, it would turn right into Second and slowly back out into Main, stopping parallel to the sidewalk. If it was running a few minutes ahead of schedule it might sit for that period of time before beginning its run up Main Street, stopping at every corner if a passenger was standing there. It would continue to Shraders Field, where it would turn around and start back towards Lynchburg down Route 29. Years later the route was extended to Thomas's Store (Thomas Motor Inn today).

When the bus crossed Williams Viaduct it would turn left down Commerce to Eighth. Traveling up Eighth it stopped at Main beside the Carroll Hotel to load and unload passengers. Continuing up Main it turned down Seventh and stopped again in the middle of the block beside Guggenheimer's Department Store (now Genworth Financial). After loading passengers it continued across the river, turned right and continued up The Old Road (Lynch's Ferry Road). When it reached Main Street, it turned right (a difficult 150 degree turn) and continued back down Main to Second Street to complete its route. There was also a Madison Heights bus that ran from Wright Shop Road to Lynchburg, but less frequently than the normal run described above. When it left Lynchburg it would travel directly up Rt. 29 and back to Wright Shop. The wrecked bus shown on the previous pages was a Wright Shop Road bus. It apparently was sideswiped by another vehicle coming down the steep hill and was knocked out of the road into the ditch on the east side of Rt. 29, a close call for the driver and passengers. Old timers will probably remember the big John P. Hughes wrecker (left above) with the words "We Pull For Lynchburg" printed on the door.

A few people owned automobiles and were able to drive to Lynchburg to shop. Occasionally they would provide rides to others. It was not unusual to be waiting for the bus and have someone come by in a car and offer you a ride to town. This kind gesture could cause trouble for the car owner if there were more people waiting than there were seats in the car because they would usually all pile in.

For those who had no car and chose not to ride the bus, the only other option was walking. Some folks walked regularly and never rode the bus. If I missed the bus by minutes I could usually walk from home to Lynchburg before the next bus ran and I frequently did. Walking alone in the daylight hours wasn't too unnerving, but nighttime was a different matter, especially if you were alone.

The section of road along the river always attracted some undesirable characters, especially in warm weather. The local people often referred to them as "winos," because they would congregate in that area and panhandle for enough money to buy a bottle of wine from the store at the end of the bridge. Once they had bought their wine they would sit under the bridge and drink it. If desperate, they would also drink what was called "canned heat" which was the alcohol-based fuel, "Sterno." I was told that they would strain the fluid through slices of bread to reduce its potential harmfulness.

I don't mean to imply that these people were fearsome criminals—they weren't. Occasionally you would see a stranger in their midst, but most of them were locals and known by everyone in the community. Many of them were World War Two veterans and some were combat survivors. They were usually harmless and polite, but there is something intimidating about walking past a group of disheveled, drunken men. I need to emphasize that I never remember them physically harming anyone except that occasionally they would harm each other.

The store at the end of the bridge still exists as The 29 Market and has had many owners. The earliest owner I remember was Hawkins. According to Oscar Mantiply, who has worked there over three decades, other owners were Charles Carter, Harold Presley, Lawrence Canada, Earl Tweedy, Bob Hart and J.A. Stevens. The early owners sold fireworks in the little addition on the right hand side of the building. They had a

The store at the end of the bridge

window that opened to the street so you could stand outside and purchase them. You could buy them most any time of year, but they were especially well stocked around Christmas. That's when we always tried to accumulate enough money to purchase them. We always called the noise makers "firecrackers" except for the little ones which we called "squibs." They were tiny little things less than an inch long. Although they had a fuse they hardly made more noise than the cap from a cap pistol. Most parents felt safe letting smaller children play with them.

Understandably, the larger they were the more noise they made and the more dangerous they were. Most of them were outlawed in Virginia many years ago. The "cherry bombs" were capable of doing real damage to flesh as well as other things. I know of one situation where one blew a commode apart in an E.C. Glass High School boy's restroom. An obvious accident, of course.

I.H. McBride Sign Co., Walter Worley's Store, and Bob Putt's house can be seen in the distance in the previous picture. The white building is McBride's, the building beyond is Worley's store and Putt's house is next. Mr. Worley lived in Bedford County, but often spent the night at the store. He would bring fresh raw milk from home and sell it at the store. He would mix you a pint of chocolate milk for a nickel. It was a favorite of many of the locals. Daddy often bought gas from him. It was a treat for me to watch him crank the handle on the side of the pump and see the gas come into the glass tank at the top. The glass had gallon marks on the side and you pumped until it reached the desired amount. He usually gave a little extra, and the gas was gravity fed into your automobile.

    As I remember Bob Putt's house it was a narrow three-story building that sat one step away from the edge of the road. Its back foundation was located over the bank and provided a third story. Glenn Meredith, a tattoo artist, lived in a small one-story building just a few feet beyond Putt's. Usually a group of men was hanging out at these houses.

Chapter 6

Attending School

People moving into Madison Heights from a more "refined" part of the world might have been shocked when they learned about our school system. First, there was no kindergarten provided by the county for preschool children. I was among the fortunate (I suppose) of my clan because I attended a kindergarten provided by someone in the community. The first place we met was in the basement of "Dr. Harris's house" on the corner of Seventh and Main. Dr. George Harris was the beloved physician of our community from 1900-1936. Since all seven of us Stinson children were born at home, I assume he delivered all of us. I never heard otherwise. I don't know why the kindergarten moved, but the second place we met was the basement of the old Odd Fellows Hall on Fourth Street between Main and Clark. Today, that building is owned by Northside Baptist Church.

I have two distinct memories from kindergarten. The first is about a "critter" and the second is about a teacher. One day while on a field trip, which was a short walk down Seventh Street behind the Harris house, I found a tiny turtle. It wasn't a box turtle, (what we called a terrapin) but looked like a miniature snapping turtle, which it probably was. The teachers tried to get me to release it. No way! I had never seen a little turtle like that before and I was determined to take it home. Even though I tried to give it the best of care, it died a few days later and I was very sad. I suppose that's why I could empathize with my sons and later my grandsons who are "critter" collectors.

Charles Stinson and Johnny Marks, 1939

My second memory regards an event that occurred after we moved to the Odd Fellows Hall. One of our teachers (she may have been a visitor or a resource person) was teaching us about music. "Does anyone know a song they can sing for us?" she asked.

"I do! I can sing '*Turkey in the straw*'."

"Good," she said, "sing it for us."

I reared back and sang it with gusto. When I finished, she informed me (and all the others) that I had sung it to the wrong tune. She then proceeded to sing it the right way (so she said). I was incensed! I was also unconvinced that she knew what she was talking about. Imagine the nerve of this stranger trying to tell me how to sing my song.

When I started school in 1941, I attended Madison Heights Elementary School on Phelps Road. Madison Heights High School was located only a few feet from the elementary school and they shared the same cafeteria, playground, and principal. In her brief history of Madison Heights schools written in 1969, Madeline Coleman noted that the High School was built in 1922. According to Lynn Cunningham, a Lynchburg architect who grew up in Madison Heights, the beautiful elementary school was built in 1939 by English Construction Company of Altavista and was one of their first major jobs.

The new elementary school replaced the one that had been built in 1912 between Seventh and Eighth Streets on the west side of Main. That school was destroyed by fire in the spring of 1938 a few months before school was over for the year. The students had an extended summer vacation, but began school on time in the new building, which

Madison Heights Elementary School

Dorothy "Tiny" Stinson's graduation, 1941. Six-year-old Charles on the left, eight-year-old Robert on the right

Three classmates walking to school Phyllis Arthur, Audrey Goff and Betty Shrader with their little friend

had already been under construction. Madeline Coleman referred to the old school as "The School on the Hill." When I was growing up, we called the vacant lot "School House Hill" and often played baseball there. Except for the high school baseball field, it was one of the few places in our hilly community where a baseball game could be held.

When I began school, I had five older siblings still attending. This provided a great sense of security for me since I was still a few months shy of my sixth birthday. You mess with the first grader, you answer to his big brothers! It also was security for three first cousins, John Marks, Massie Stinson, and Raymond Stinson, who began school with me. All four of us graduated in 1953. Since Amherst County provided no transportation to school for Madison Heights children, we normally walked the mile to school. Young people today laugh at us "old timers" talking about how far we had to walk to school and some insist we claim, "It was uphill both ways."

We were classified as "walkers," and as such were the first to be released in the afternoon, a real plus! Sometimes during inclement weather we would ride the bus to school, but not always. The severity of the weather and the availability of funds usually determined whether we rode or walked. When it was raining hard we were more likely to ride the bus. There were never enough umbrellas to go around so we would crowd under one if possible and hurry to shelter on somebody's front porch to wait for the bus.

Snowy days were different. Schools seldom closed for snow unless it was very deep, but many children stayed home anyway to sleigh ride or build snowmen. Walking to school in the snow was an adventure and snowball battles were plentiful. We didn't dread it nearly as much as we did a cold, rainy day.

MRS. WOODSON'S SEVENTH GRADE CLASS
Left to right, front row: Massie Stinson, Earl Clarkson, Jimmie Turner, Alfred Bryant, J.T. Banton, Jack Martin, Joan Hunt, Joyce Hunt, Amy Martin, Audrey Goff, Ray Watts. Second row: Charles Stinson Third Row: Shirley Freeman, Peggy Peters, Betty Gail Eggleston, Joan Barker, Jewel Vest, Doris Patterson, Myrtle Tomlin, unknown, unknown. Fourth row: Esthmus Carson, Lloyd Lee, unknown, Withers Whitehead, Betty Ayers, Jessee Hartless, Addie Cyrus, George Wilkerson with Howard Proffitt standing in front of him. Back row: Mrs. Glenmore Woodson, Ray Campbell, Loretta, Loretta Hudson, Marjorie Hartless, Dorothy Doss, Floyd Whitehead.

There was still adventure to be had on our daily treks even when it wasn't snowing. I was in the second grade when some of my classmates (one of them might have been me) came up with the idea one afternoon of smoking "monkey cigars." For the uninformed, these are the dried, foot-long seedpods from the catalpa tree. They are also called by other colloquial names such as "Indian cigars." Charlie Goff, one of the Madison Heights bus drivers, had a large tree in his yard. We bought two small boxes of wooden stem matches for a penny at Raymond Woody's store. Five or six of us had a grand old time puffing those things and pretending it was great fun. In reality, the harsh smoke felt like it was taking the skin off my tongue. We were so busy "having fun" that we failed to see the car filled with teachers from our school as they passed by, but they saw us.

The next day, all the villains were rounded up to pay for their awful deed. The penalty was this: The offenders would be paraded to every class room in the elementary school and made to stand in front of each class while their horrible action was described to everyone. (I wonder how this would go over today?) Somehow I escaped the initial

MRS. QUIGLEY'S SEVENTH GRADE CLASS
Left to right, front row: Marilyn Dewitt, Anne Rosser, Copey Jones, Connie Gouyer, Jean Bryant, Phyllis Arthur, Betty Shrader, Dorothy Blanks, Betty Lou Stinnett and Betty Hostetter. Second row: Billy Ogden, Carrol Bryant, Leroy Shaner, John Marks, Dean White, Jack Hartless, Ann McGann, Raymond Stinson, Richard Campbell, Dale Spradlin. Third row: Juanita Hughes, Doris Blunke, Shirley Hughes, unknown, unknown, Don Adams, unknown, Marion "Pete" Abbitt. Fourth row: Everett Coleman, Ruby Nash, unknown, Lois Hubbard, Bobby Woody, Franklin "Chick" Cooper, Mrs. Quigley, Jimmy Nuckols and Bernard Blanks. (This 36-member class combined with the other seventh grade class on the previous page became the class of 1953, which graduated 59 members)

identification process. All the other boys were rounded up. As they prepared to leave, the teacher asked, "Were any of the rest of you boys involved in this?" Surely she didn't think I was dumb enough to confess? Just as they were leaving the room, my old buddy Albert (not his real name…may he rest in peace) said, "Charles was smoking them too." The teacher instructed me to take my place with the rabble. I have never been so humiliated in my life. When we entered each of the eleven rooms and stood in front of the class, I never took my eyes off my feet. I didn't see anyone in the classes, but they all saw me. My brother Robert was in one class and my sister Margaret was in another. Robert had a bicycle that he rode to school that day and he set a record going home to tell Mama the news. She was waiting for me when I got home. End of story. (Not really.)

The second shocking lesson that a newcomer to Madison Heights may learn was that there was no eighth grade in our school system. As noted already, in terms of distance, the high school was just a few steps away from the elementary school. In

Walkers, left to right, left photo: Barbara Ray, Patsy Perdue, Barbara Wright
Right photo: Nancy Campbell, Julia Manley

Left to right: Walter Apperson, Jerome Cooper Cecil Banton, Frank Taliaferro

Corrine Tyree

Left: unknown
Right: Roy Eggleston

terms of promotion, when we completed the seventh grade we went right into high school, graduating after eleven years of schooling. Don't ask me why. I didn't analyze it, I just rejoiced over it. My transition from seventh grade to high school was a simple matter of changing halls in the same building.

    Mrs. Glenmore Woodson was one of my favorite teachers. I only remember her getting mad once and that was my fault. We would tightly-roll pieces of paper and bend them in a V-shape and shoot them with a rubber band. Although we never spit on them, we called them "spitballs." Mrs. Woodson was at the blackboard teaching beside a large pull-down map. She had her back turned and I shot a "spitball" at a boy across the aisle in front of me. I missed. The "spitball" kept traveling and hit the map right beside her head. She was furious! I stuck the rubber band in my shoe. She tried every way she knew to find out who shot it, but nobody would confess. After it was over, the boy behind me whispered, "You can take that rubber band out of your shoe now." I owe him one.

Most of the members of the class of 1953 were seventeen when we graduated, but some were only sixteen. Apparently our education wasn't inferior to others who had completed twelve years because many of my classmates excelled in their chosen fields. The students who were "walkers" were primarily those who had access to the sidewalk or lived close to the school. All the walkers in this chapter lived in Old Town Madison Heights.

Several other high schools were scattered throughout the county and numerous elementary schools. When the children completed elementary school in their communities they were then bussed to the closest High School. Students from Galt's Mill, Stapleton, Wright Shop Road, Pedlar Mills, Elon, Pleasant View, and Monroe were all brought to Madison Heights High School.

This 1948 baseball team was undefeated. Not only were they one of the best, but also one of the largest. What attracted so many guys to the team and motivated them to become champions? I think it was the coach (see next page).

A newcomer to our community might have experienced a further shock when they learned we had no gymnasium at our school. Obviously this was a big hindrance

MADISON HEIGHTS BASEBALL TEAM, 1948
Left to right, front: Wendell Overstreet, Glenn Ricketts, Maynard Wood, Gerald Thomas with catcher John "Sonny Boy" Walker seated on the ground in front of him, Landrum Humphreys, Henry "Sonny" Robertson, Calvin Burford.
Back: Bobby Floyd, Clayton Wright, Billy Woody, N.J. Thomas, Ezra Humphreys, Linwood Coleman, Lewis Rhodes, Robert Ewers, and Paul Campbell.

Coach Annabelle Watts, 1948

Bus from Colony Road High School, 1947

to our limited sports program, especially our basketball team which played their home games at the Lynchburg YMCA. Basketball and baseball were the only sports we competed in with other schools. The size of each team was necessarily small because we had so few students. In 1953, there were 59 members in my graduating class, 12 members on the boys' basketball team, 14 on the girls' team, and only 12 on the baseball team which had to keep nine players on the field at all times. This was an improvement over the 10-member baseball team of the previous year. Our Physical Education Director, Richard Tanner, was coach for all the teams. As astonishing as this may sound to those involved in our sophisticated high school programs today, there is much to be said for the old way in which we played sports. Today, only the best get to play.

Because Madison Heights High School graduates were predominately from three areas, Monroe, Elon, and Madison Heights, Miss Mary Gordon Harris coined a word using all three of these localities: **MON-EL-ISON**. In 1930, it became the name of the school yearbook, which had been started in 1926 by Thomas Banton. (This information was printed in the *1940 MONELISON* in a paragraph on page 47 called "DID YOU KNOW THAT—.")

Before the schools were integrated, black students from Madison Heights were educated at a school on Colony Road that was also called Madison Heights Elementary and High School. Some black students from outlying areas were also bussed daily to that school. After segregation ended, the school

1953 GIRLS BASKEBALL TEAM
Left to right, front row: Carolyn Lee, Patsy Lee, Shelby Floyd, Phyllis Arthur, Bettie Crews, and Marie Wood. Second row: Loretta Sanders, Pat McGann, Ellen Cash, Juanita Hartless, Anita Ewers, Eleanor Lee, Beverly Puckett, Kathryn Proffitt, Richard Tanner, coach.

on Colony Road became known as James River Elementary School.

The American school scene changed drastically in the early 1960s with the advent of centralized high schools, desegregation, and mass bussing. Some of these changes came to Amherst County even earlier with the construction of one central high school near the town of Amherst in 1955-56. The first classes started attending the new school in the 1956-57 school year. The transition to one central high school took several years to complete and Madison Heights High School continued to operate until it graduated its last class in 1962.

Barry McBride, a member of the final graduating class, retold a story told by Donald Layne at a recent class reunion. Layne was a new teacher hired during the final years of operation who became the basketball, baseball, soccer, and volleyball coach. Layne's version of the story went something like this: He was first interviewed for the teaching position and then told, "We want you to be our basketball coach too."

"I suppose I can do that. Where is your gymnasium?"

"It's out back."

"I was just out there and all I saw was a parking lot."

"That's our gym. We want you to coach baseball also."

"Where's the baseball field?"

Class Of 1952
Left to right
Front row: Ollie Mae Stowe, Geraldine Brown, Joyce Bryant, Shirley Connelly, Nancy Cash, Jeane Tyree, Bessie Davis, Mary Lou Phillips, Barbara Oliver, Arlene Campbell, Corrine Tyree, Barbara Wiley, Marion Johnson, June Young, Virginia Padgett, Julia Manley, Shirley Woody, Evelyn Davis, Barbara Moore.
Second row: Sandra Mccraw, Shirley Dean, Anna Belle Moore, Doris Brown, Janice Brown, Corinne Garvin, Tillie Terry, Judy Moss, Peggy Taylor, Marilyn Hostetter, June Simmons, Rosalie Burford, Nancy Campbell, Dorothy Baldwin, Wanda Moss, Cecil Humphries, Jean Burch, Connie Stinnette, Christine Thornton, Lila McBride.
Third row: Shirley Coleman, Shirley Banton, Peggy Shrader, Margaret Franklin, Glenna Langley, Dewey Ripley, Charles Knowles, Jimmy Steuart, Lawrence Cooper, Homer Massie, Bill Nixon, James Davis, Terry Staton, Charles Newcomb, Harold Pugh, Polly Wilkerson, Jean Shaner.
Fourth row: Donald Ewers, Richard Blount, James Story, Russell Burford, Thomas Burford, George Farish, Richard Nicholas, Lester Harris, Douglas Morcom, Arnold Ewers, Gordon Overstreet.

"Behind the gym."

Surprisingly, the new teacher accepted the position and according to McBride led the basketball team to victory over the new and larger Amherst County High School team in both of the scheduled games in the final year.

Like most of the other local high schools that were closed, the vacated buildings at Madison Heights High School were used for other school related purposes for a time. The Madison Heights Elementary School and High School buildings were combined and renovated to become Seminole Elementary School for many years before closing their doors for the final time in 1991. While some of the old county school buildings have been disposed of, the two large facilities on Phelps Road sit unused and deteriorating. This has served as a source of great agitation for the

Madison Heights High School

decreasing numbers of us who passed through their halls more than half a century ago and remember their glory days.

The good news is that at the time of this writing, plans are being developed to restore these buildings to their former splendor. A combined effort by Amherst County leaders, concerned alumni, and private enterprise is aimed at reestablishing these buildings as teaching facilities whose graduates will become known worldwide for their skills. May it come to pass soon!

OUR ALMA MATER

By the James in Amherst County
Beautiful to see
Proudly stands our Alma Mater
Dear to you and me
Through the years
We've worked together
We have blazed a trail
So – to thee, our Alma Mater
MADISON HIGH – all Hail!

HAIL TO THE BLUE AND GOLD
(SCHOOL SONG)

Hail to the Blue and Gold
And the School whose colors we are wearing
They're thrilling to behold
When the Team defending them wins again,
So march on to victory
While the School is cheering us onward
Shout and sing–
Let the heavens ring–
With the song for MADISON HEIGHTS!

by Rev. Ernest E. Emurian
Pastor of Madison Heights Baptist Church, 1941–47

Chapter 7

In Case of Emergency…

When I was growing up in Madison Heights, we had limited resources to respond to emergencies and depended heavily on Lynchburg for those services. An outsider might have engaged a local in the following conversation.

"Do you people ever have an emergency, like a house fire?"

"Sure."

"What do you do?"

"Send someone to a telephone to call the Lynchburg Fire Department while we try to put the fire out."

"Where's a telephone?"

"The neighbor in the next block has one. They don't mind if other people use it."

"What's the number for the Fire Department?"

"We don't need a number, you just pick the phone up and tell the operator, she'll call them for you."

"What do you do if you need an ambulance?"

"Same thing. She'll call Whitten Funeral Home or Diuguid Funeral Home, they'll send one."

"Why would she call a funeral home?"

"They operate the ambulances for the city."

"What about a policeman?"

Ed Childress Madison Square Market 1949 Whitten Funeral Home calendar advertising "Ambulance Service 24 Hours Daily"

"Same thing. Just tell her who to call. She can call the State Police, the County Sheriff, or Mr. Justis."

"Who is Mr. Justis?"

"The Town Constable."

"Justis? Is that really his name?"

"Yep."

As strange as the above may seem, that's the way it was until things slowly began to change after World War II.

When the funeral homes decided to get out of the non-profit ambulance business during the 1950s, the city first tried to contract the services out to private providers, but this did not prove satisfactory. At one time the ambulances were operated by one of the cab companies who already had drivers on call 24 hours a day. When an ambulance arrived during this era, it was staffed by a funeral home employee or a taxi driver depending on the service provider. You hoped he had received some first aid training. Their job primarily was to get you into the ambulance and make a run for Lynchburg General Hospital. (The concept of training emergency medical technicians (EMT) did not exist until about 1971.)

Fatal fire on Seventh Street, Easter Sunday, 1951

Monelison Volunteer Fire Department

Lynchburg's ambulance service went through years of turmoil beginning in the 1950s that culminated with the Fire Department taking over all the emergency medical services. Because the fire and rescue services were paid for with city monies, calls outside the city limits were billed to the recipients. This obviously was fair, but it also was expensive. During these changing times, volunteer fire and rescue companies began to organize to meet the needs of the fast growing suburban areas. Monelison Volunteer Fire Department (Note the name) was formed in 1959 and located near the intersection of Rt. 29 and Rt. 130.

Doctor visits were different in those days too; they made house calls. Well, not all the time, but if you were really sick they would come see you. I remember having strep throat once and being delirious with a temperature of 104 degrees. Dr. Oscar Ramsey came to my house and gave me a shot of penicillin. I was soon well. I was one of the fortunate ones. I remember many years later standing at the grave of a boy who had died from strep throat when he was eight years old. The discovery of penicillin came a few years too late for him.

During annual flu outbreaks the doctors would work hard tending people in their offices during the day and in the homes after office hours. I remember the elderly widow of one Lynchburg doctor telling me about such a time in her husband's life. She said, "Every time he came home and went to bed the phone would ring again. He would answer it, get up and leave again. This had gone on for several days and he was exhausted. When he came home one evening in time for supper, he was so happy to sit down with our son and me to eat. He bowed his head to ask the blessing and when he closed his eyes he said, 'Hello.' My son and I burst out in uncontrollable laughter. He got very mad at both of us!"

We had a telephone before many of our neighbors did so people often came to our house to use the phone. Most people were thankful for the privilege and considerate of time constraints, making their calls brief. During World War II and for many years following, a normal long distance call was for three minutes. Additional minutes were expensive and sometimes not available. It was quite an ordeal to have operators try to connect calls across the country. Pity the poor serviceman during war time who was trying to get in a call home before shipping overseas, not knowing if he would ever return. He could wait for hours for a phone, try desperately to get a call through, and if successful, be cut off at the end of three minutes before he could speak to everyone. The operator would usually interrupt and tell you that you had "thirty seconds left." It happened often.

Private lines were difficult to get and expensive. Four-party lines were impossible to live with. Two-party lines were not too bad if you had a good second party. How did you know if your neighbor was using the phone? You picked it up and heard them talking so you quietly hung it up. That was the proper thing to do. Did it happen all the time? What do you think? You had to be careful what you said on a party line.

Party lines usually had a suffix. Our number was 6464-R and our neighbor on our two-party line was 6464-J. When we wanted to make a call, regardless of what kind of line we had, we simply picked up the phone, the operator would say, "Number please," and we would give her the number. (Yes it was always "her." There were no male operators.) Operators would also give you the time if you asked them. We kids drove them crazy picking the phone up and saying, "could

1948-1949 C&P Telephone Directory

you give me the correct time please?" They always obliged.

Eventually, private lines became available to most everyone, but some folks were slow to change because it cost more. It's amazing what some folks will endure for money! Not many years passed before we had the dialing system. In the early days when there were not so many phones, there was no need for seven digit numbers. For example, an ad placed in our 1953 MONELSION yearbook by CANADA PRODUCE COMPANY said Dial 2-3483. This indicates the dial system was in place, but only 5 digit numbers were needed. Our first seven-digit exchange was called "Victor" with the VI representing 84. An example would be "My telephone number is Victor 5-7934." Soon Victor ceased to be used and the number evolved into 845-7934. Later, as the phone system expanded, the 846 and 847 prefixes were needed. These three prefixes are still the common numbers in Madison Heights and downtown Lynchburg.

Although I never saw an old wall-mounted crank phone in Madison Heights, (the kind you see in antique stores today), they were still being used in some places in Virginia in the late 1940s and early 1950s. When my brother Earl moved his family to Lexington in 1948, they rented an apartment in a Rockbridge County farmhouse about five miles outside of town. That house was equipped with an old wooden crank phone and was still being used when they moved away in 1952. When you cranked it, everyone on the line was alerted that someone was making a call. Curiosity prevailed. A visit to the Museum in Scottsville, Virginia will let you listen to a simulated phone call on an old crank phone in which an eavesdropper is confronted with "I know you're listening like you always do, now hang up!"

PART THREE:

People, Places and Animals

Chapter 8

John Mayberry and the Monkey

Two Mayberry families were especially close friends with my family. Elmer Mayberry's family lived on Clark Street and his brother John and his family lived on the James River. John's home was torn down when the Route 29 bypass was built around Lynchburg in 1954 and the family moved into the house formerly owned by Elijah Ennis on Horseford Road. Both Mayberry families had children who were close in age to my brothers and sisters. I was the youngest of the 24 children in the three families.

My closest neighbors were an elderly couple, Jessee and Cora Tyree (picture in Chapter Two), who frequently called on one of my siblings or me to help them with some chore. Mrs. Tyree was sister to John Mayberry's wife, Belle, and liked to visit with her occasionally. When she would go for a visit to their home on the river, she would get one of us children to walk with her. The trip consisted of a walk down Horseford Road, down Dark Hollow and down the river road to the Mayberry house. She would visit with her sister and then we would return home. She always paid us a quarter to accompany her.

On one such trip, I was visiting with Mr. Mayberry on their large front porch while Mrs. Tyree and her sister were inside talking. Mr. Mayberry was usually a talkative person, but on this particular day he appeared quiet and distracted. I was anxious to talk to him about a monkey that I'd heard had mysteriously appeared on his property, but he acted like he didn't want to talk about it. I didn't understand why.

John and Belle Mayberry
50th Wedding Anniversary, 1955

At various times, some of his sons worked for either Conner Produce or Canada Produce in Lynchburg. They would often bring home old produce and dump it on the riverbank several hundred feet from the house. While sitting on the porch one day, Mr. Mayberry saw a monkey swim across the river and begin eating some of the old bananas on the riverbank. When he approached the monkey it ran into the woods on the hillside behind the house. In the days following, it returned frequently to eat from the produce pile. Mr. Mayberry was determined to trap the monkey. He built a large framed trap, covered it with chicken wire, and built a drop door like one on a rabbit trap. (You know what they look like, right?) He sat it on the barn roof and baited it with enticing monkey food…nice ripe bananas.

Mrs. Tyree and I had heard about the monkey and stopped to examine the trap when we walked by. As a curious young teenager, I was anxious to learn all I could about the monkey and was asking Mr. Mayberry one question after another as we sat together on the porch. I got the impression that he was wishing I would shut up, go away, or both. I was really confused by his actions and my inability to communicate with him. Suddenly he jumped to his feet and screamed, "I caught the monkey!" I almost fell backwards off the porch. The two women came rushing outside and we all hurried away to see the monkey.

Needless to say, the monkey was frantic because of the trap and the four people peering in at him. Mr. Mayberry was elated and resumed his old talkative way as he began telling his story. "I saw the monkey when he came down from the woods and went to the trap. I was afraid the boy (that's me) would see him and scare him away. Finally, he went in. When I saw the door fall down, I knew I had him!" I know nothing

The mysterious monkey

about monkeys, but I remember him being about 18 to 24 inches tall. While I was searching through old photos in Madison Heights I came across a picture of a monkey in a cage built of chicken wire. I'm not certain that it's the same monkey, but I've never heard of anyone else there having a monkey, so I've decided to include it.

News spread fast about the monkey and many people came to see him and hear Mr. Mayberry's story. People offered many theories about where the monkey came from, but nobody ever knew. One day a visitor who had been drinking too much decided he was going to "tame" the monkey. When he opened the cage, the monkey escaped and quickly disappeared in the woods. He was never seen again.

Since I'm writing about the Mayberry clan, I suppose this would be the time to tell another story about one of them. One of John Mayberry's sons was called "Johnny Man." He was a handsome, fun-loving, gregarious young man with a devil-may-care attitude who was loved by everyone. He was extremely strong for his slight build. When he was going home at night from visiting in Madison Heights he would walk down Horseford Road, which was behind our house. When he walked he would whistle. In the summer time we would often hear him whistling as he walked home in the dark. I've heard that people do that as a fear tactic, but it's hard to imagine "Johnny Man" being afraid of anything.

Dark Hollow was the name given to the pathway from Horseford Road to the River Road. It ran between two very steep hills. There were many rock ledges like steps along the descending trail. One dark night, a cow had lain down behind one of those ledges. As "Johnny Man" came whistling along in the dark, he stepped out on the cow's back and she jumped up and bellowed. He never told us the rest of the story.

"Johnny Man" was the same age as my oldest brother, Frank, so they were drafted into the army at the same time during World War II. Draftees were given a date and time to report to Amherst and from there they would be sent to Roanoke for processing. After Frank finished high school in 1940, he had taken a job at Dahlgren, Virginia at the Naval Weapons Proving Grounds and worked there until he was drafted. "Johnny Man" came to our house and asked Daddy if he could ride to Amherst with him when

"Johnny Man" Mayberry

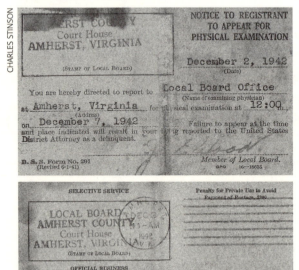

1942 Draft Card

he took Frank, and of course Daddy was glad to give him a ride. On the morning they were scheduled to leave, one of the children looked out the window and said, "Here comes 'Johnny Man' riding a mule!"

Everyone ran outside.

"Where'd you get that mule?" asked one of my brothers.

"I found him walking around over on Horseford Road."

"Do you know who he belongs to?"

"Nope. Never seen him before."

"What you gonna do with him?"

"I'm gonna ride him to the Army!"

Since nobody under the age of 55 has ever received one of these cards I thought it might be good to show what one looked like. Many young men lived in the fear of getting drafted, especially in wartime. Unless there were physical or mental reasons for a person not serving they were usually drafted into the military unless there were other special reasons they could be deferred or exempted. This is my brother Frank's card that he received while working for the government at Dahlgren, Virginia. He served with MacArthur in the Philippines and was one of the last to return after the war.

NICKNAMES

Like most communities, many of our people had nicknames. You've already been introduced to a few of them and I've refrained from using some others. It's uncommon to find a picture like the one above where everyone has an unusual nickname. Meet "Chat" Mayberry, "Boots" Tyree, and "Johnny Man" Mayberry (left to right). I don't know how the last two got their moniker, but "Chat" was short for Chattaroy, a name given him by his daddy. The story I've heard was that John Mayberry, who worked on the railroad, saw the name written on a boxcar and decided to bestow it upon his next child if the baby was a boy. Although Chat was eight years older than me, he became a wonderful friend and a great fishing buddy.

CHAPTER 9

Bill Layne and his Dog Bruce

You met Bill Layne in Chapter Four and learned about his work at "The Foundry." Like many other Madison Heights men, Bill's life was interrupted during World War II by a call to serve his country in the military. Bill had a beautiful collie dog named Bruce. When Bill learned that he was going to be drafted he decided to allow Bruce to enter the military also since the Army was badly in need of dogs for their Quartermaster Canine Corps. Some dogs were trained for combat services while others were trained to serve as sentry dogs on Army posts.

Bill and Bruce

Whether dogs would be allowed to return to their owners depended on the type of training they received. Bill and Bruce went off to war.

Bill was in Battery "B" of the 497th Antiaircraft Artillery Battalion and ended up in the Pacific Theatre, serving on Guadalcanal and then "island hopping" to the Philippine Islands. Bruce stayed stateside and served in Oklahoma and Kentucky as a sentry dog. After the war, Bill's family received notification that Bruce could return home if they wanted him and they did. He was

Bessie Layne and Bruce

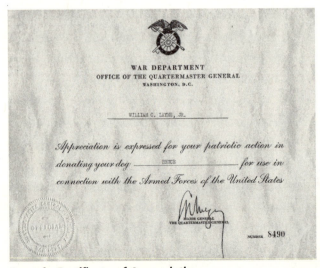

Bruce's Certificate of Appreciation

shipped by train to Lynchburg and returned to Stumps Hill where he waited for his master to return from overseas.

Bessie Layne was Bill's sister who lived in the Layne home place. When Bruce returned home from the service, Bessie brought him home and took care of him until Bill returned from the war.

I was ten years old when Bruce was released from the Army. He had been trained to always walk, stand, or sit on the left side of the soldier who carried his rifle on the right. The children in the community quickly learned of Bruce's training. Bruce had the freedom to wander about the community where we lived and when he showed up where we were playing we would always put him to the test. It was great sport for us to go stand on the "wrong side" of the dog and see him move around to the opposite side. The poor dog never got any rest when we were around. He probably would have liked to practice some of his "attack training" on the seat of our pants, but he never did. He was a great dog.

Several years after Bill and Bruce were reunited, Bruce was struck by a motorcycle and died

Bill and his friend Franklin, Guadalcanal, World War II

from the injuries he received.

All four of the men shown below returned home safely after the war, but all of the servicemen from our community were not so fortunate. Three of my neighbors were killed in the war. Two marines, James L. Adams from Third Street and Garland Ricketts from Church Street died in major battles in Pacific Campaigns. Garland was killed by a land mine on March 8, 1945 during the Battle of Iwo Jima. James was killed by machine gun fire on May 10, 1945 during the Battle of Okinawa.

Garland and Bill Layne both attended the Methodist Church. Recently when discussing his wartime experiences, Bill became very emotional when discussing Garland's death. "One of the most difficult things I've ever had to do was go back to church for the first time after I came home and face Mrs. Ricketts. I felt so guilty. I was

Bill Layne, Virgil Coleman

George Martin

Walter Freeman

Bill Layne, George Martin, Virgil Coleman, and Walter Freeman were four men from Madison Heights who served together in the 497th Antiaircraft Artillery Battalion. Bill and George served in Battery B. Virgil and Walter were in Battery A.

still alive, but her son was dead." Guilt was only one of the emotional scars that some of our young men brought home from the war. Like other war veterans, most of them talked very little about their experiences or the pain it caused. At least five World War II veterans that I knew from our community became alcoholics. There may have been others. After their deaths, stories circulated about some of them and war related causes that led to their drinking. I doubt if anyone will ever know for sure. I suspect their secrets lie buried with them. The third man from Madison Heights that I remember being killed in the war was William Sligh. He was in the Army and was killed in Europe during the Battle of the Bulge, the bloodiest battle that U.S. forces experienced in World War II. It was Hitler's last offensive and lasted from December 16, 1944 until January 25, 1945. William was a native of Big Island, but married Marion Brightwell who lived at 206 Main Street. Their son, James "Jimmy" Sligh, was born in August 1943 before William shipped overseas in December. William was wounded and captured by the Germans. A comrade who was also captured wrote Marion to tell about William's final days. He said, "We had no food, no blankets, no medicine and no fuel, but they are still fighting." William died 16 days before the war ended.

Garland Ricketts

James L. Adams

William Sligh

JIMMY SLIGH AND VIRGINIA WOOD
Jimmy was the son of William Sligh whose story is told on the previous page. Virginia Wood was one of the organizers of the annual Poppy Day sale held on Memorial Day weekend (See chapter 20). In the 1949 sale, five-year old Jimmy was chosen to present one of the first poppies to Mrs. Wood in memory of his father who died in World War Two.

Chapter 10

Plowmen and Their Horses

Almost everyone in Madison Heights raised a vegetable garden. I'm not talking about the small Victory Gardens that people were encouraged to plant during World War II. A more appropriate name for our garden would have been a Survival Garden because it provided a large part of the food throughout the year for our family of nine. We lived on a 2.37-acre lot and some years almost half of it was planted in garden. Although we shared some of our excess with neighbors, Mama canned everything she could. Although we didn't like it, all of us children worked in the garden.

Because of the size of our gardens it was necessary to have them plowed with a horse. Our main garden, as well as some others in the area, was not accessible with a tractor. There were two people in old Madison Heights that plowed with horses, Johnny Hesson and James Cash.

When you live in a small community you usually know everyone who lives there. In the eyes of a child some people appear

An unknown plowman and his horse

Bob Ricketts, Johnny Hesson

to be ancient and unchanging. Mr. Johnny Hesson was one of those people. I'm sure I would be surprised if I knew how old he was when he was plowing gardens in Madison Heights, but he was probably younger than he appeared to me. Mr. Hesson lived on Fifth Street next door to the Methodist Church. He had a barn beside his house where he kept his horse and a small pasture behind the barn. The house and barn have been torn down. It wasn't uncommon to see him walking along our streets with his horse dragging a wooden sled that he used to carry his plow and harrow. Some sleds even had seats, but most drivers walked alongside holding the reins.

When plowing time came, daddy would always take note of the ground and monitor the dampness so it wouldn't be plowed when it was too wet. When he felt the time was right, he would contact Mr. Hesson to plow for him. I remember going with Daddy to talk with him about plowing. As Mr. Hesson grew older, it became increasingly more difficult for him to continue plowing and eventually he quit.

James Cash stood in contrast to Johnny Hesson in age. He was just a teenager when he started plowing gardens. As an only child, James was no stranger to hard work on the family homestead. Besides the horse, his family had other farm animals to care for and most of the responsibility was his from a very early age. One of his duties was to lead the horse to a nearby creek for water. James was several years older than I was, but I considered him my good friend and visited with him often. Frequently he would let me ride on the horse while he led him to water. I was always afraid I was going to slide down the horse's neck when he leaned down to drink. Although James was very young when he began plowing our garden he always did a good job. He was well-mannered and very conscientious, traits that pleased my daddy.

It was always entertaining for us children to watch the powerful animal pull the plow deeply through the rich soil, turning it over into huge curls in the garden. We would follow along examining any rocks or other items turned up by the plow and then scatter out of the way as the horse made a return trip. Sometimes we would find "clay marbles" that we called "dirt peas." Although they varied in size, they were usually smaller and lighter than our marbles. They were no good for playing marbles, which we did frequently, but we still treasured them because they were ancient and mysterious. I've since learned that playing marbles dates back to prehistoric times. Historians divide the evolution of the marble into three broad groups according to the material: Stone, followed by clay, and later glass. Clay marbles were used by Native Americans and colonial Americans. Which group played games with the ones we found? I wish I knew.

Playing marbles was a much loved form of recreation when I was a boy. As in most games, some boys became more proficient than others. Generally speaking, a circle was drawn in the dirt with a sharp rock or stick. Each player placed an equal number of marbles in the center of the ring and took turns shooting. If you knocked one or more marbles out of the ring, you kept shooting until you failed to do so, then the next player took a turn. If you were "playing for keeps" (which most of our mothers disapproved of, but the boys did anyway) you kept all the marbles you knocked out of the ring. If you were "playing for fun" you gave the marbles back. Boys could identify their own marbles like a shepherd could his sheep! It wasn't unusual to see a boy with his pockets bulging, holes in the knees of his pants, and the toes of his shoes ruined. Mothers really disapproved of that. It should be noted that shooting rules were often negotiated for each game and varied widely. A few years ago my great-nephew came to visit me from out of town. The ten-year-old had some marbles and wanted me to shoot with him. He had his own rules for playing a game inside on the carpet. I took great joy in winning his marbles, but my wife made me give them back to him. He wouldn't play me anymore.

Today's generation cannot comprehend how seriously we took our marble playing. Cities participated in national marble tournaments. Lewis R. Raasch was an older friend of mine who grew up in Lynchburg. He was the runner up in the Marble Championship for the city playgrounds in 1937 and came back to win in 1939. He was presented the two medals shown on the next page by radio station WLVA.

Lewis was transported in style to New Orleans in a new automobile furnished by one of the Lynchburg auto dealers to compete in the

Boy playing marbles

National Marble Tournament. Lewis, who was 13, was proud to represent his city, but greatly humiliated when he lost. He said, "The kid that beat me was only about nine or ten years old."

One thing that amazes me is that while we found clay marbles in the Madison Heights dirt, I only remember finding one arrowhead. While some excellent relics have been found in other parts of Amherst County they seemed to be scarce in our community. I suppose that almost 200 years of continuously gardening the land contributed to that.

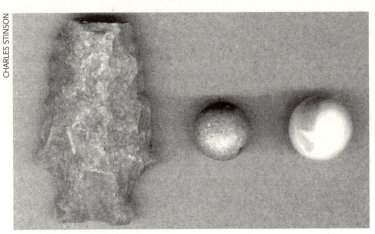

Relics
Left to right
Arrowhead, clay marble, glass marble

Years ago, some Bedford County farm families in the area where I now live would hunt arrowheads in their newly plowed fields for Sunday afternoon entertainment. Their efforts were rewarded with some excellent collections. Sadly, many of the farms and the family owned collections have now disappeared. Today, plowed fields are scarce and new forms of entertainment occupy people's time on Sunday afternoon.

Lewis Raasch Medals 1937 and 1939
The back of the 1937 medal on the left reads "RUNNER UP MARBLE CHAMPIONSHIP AWARDED BY WLVA." The back of the 1939 medal on the right reads "PLAYGROUND CHAMPION MARBLE TOURNAMENT AWARDED BY WLVA."

Chapter 11

Samuel E. "Sam" Tyree

Since purchasing the *Amherst County Virginia Heritage* books, *Volumes I and II*, I occasionally sit down and read selected articles from them. I recently read again the information on the Sam Tyree family in *Volume II* that covered four generations beginning with him. I remember all four generations. His son Marvin lived only a few blocks from us. I remember his untimely death at age 55. His children were in the same age range as my siblings and me.

Sam Tyree was a retired N & W railroad man who lived to be nearly 82 years old. He was brother to Jesse Tyree, my neighbor, pictured in chapter two. He lived near the James River and used a boat to go to work on Percival's Island. He still kept one many years after he retired. When he went to Lynchburg he walked by the river road or went by boat. When he came to the Post Office or one of the Madison Heights stores he would always walk the footpath to lower Clark Street. That area was one of the favorite playing places for my siblings, my cousins, our friends who lived close by, and me. Consequently, there were usually a lot of children around and Mr. Tyree knew this. One of his favorite games was to sneak up on us unobserved and then pretend he was going to catch us. As we scattered like a covey of quail he would scream out to us, "Come back here! If I catch you, I'm gonna pin your ears back, grease you up real good and swallow you whole!" There wasn't a child in the crowd that didn't believe he could do it. We were as afraid of him as we were a bear. Some of the little children never stopped running until they were safely home with their

FOUR GENERATIONS OF TYREES, 1950
Left to right Mr. "Sam" Tyree, Marvin Tyree, Albert "Bunk" Tyree, and his son Marshall Lee "Butch" Tyree.

mamas. As you can imagine, most of the mothers didn't appreciate Mr. Tyree's humor. As soon as the older children were safely out of reach, they would stop and begin to taunt him, knowing he couldn't outrun them. I think he enjoyed that too. The braver ones would run daringly close to him and some would even call him names. They knew better than to use "cuss words" because their parents would have never tolerated that so they created new names for him. Standing well out of range, they would yell at him and call him names. He would lunge at them like he was coming after them and they would run like crazy! Eventually, he would continue his journey and we would go back to playing, but since we knew he would be returning, we always stayed alert.

One day, he caught my sister Margaret and told her he was going to "bite her ears off." She was scared and screaming. My brother Earl did what all of us kids did when we were threatened, he grabbed a rock. Rocks, the oldest of weapons, are still effective in a competent hand. We grew up hearing people make comments like, "He's death with a rock!" (Translated, that means, "You don't want him throwing one at you.") Earl came to the rescue of his little sister. He threw the rock and struck Mr. Tyree on the knee, sending him to the ground. Earl and Margaret ran for their lives towards home. Mr. Tyree got to his feet and hobbled down the path to our house to tell Mama that Earl had hit him with a rock. Mama already knew about Mr. Tyree's "game" and Earl got there first to tell his side of the story. Mama was waiting on the porch with broom in hand when Mr. Tyree arrived. She had a way of cutting through the fluff, and told Mr. Tyree plainly, "You got exactly what you deserved." Later on he was overheard telling someone to "watch out for that little hellion over there (referring to Earl), he'll hit you with a rock."

When I was older, my friends and I would go to the river fishing and sometimes stop to visit Mr. Tyree. We found him to be fun to talk to and very accommodating. We would sit with him on the porch and talk or drink water from his well. Once, two of my teen-age friends, Raymond Stinson and Lloyd Gunter, discovered that a grove of beech trees in Magazine Hollow, which was behind his house, was filled with squirrels. Mr. Tyree loaned them his ten-gauge shotgun and shells and they killed some squirrels and gave them to him. The kick from that gun made a big impression on both of them and gave Lloyd a bloody nose! Sam Tyree had a lot of fun scaring us kids when we were little, but he left us some great memories in the process.

Chapter 12

Edwin "Buzzy" McBride

We were eating supper when our dogs began barking, alerting us that somebody was coming.

"It's Buzzy," I said, as I looked out the window. In just a minute, our paperboy was knocking at the door.

"Come in Buzzy," said my mom.

"I want to collect for the paper," said Buzzy as he handed mom the paper.

"I thought I just paid you," teased my dad.

"That was last week," smiled Buzzy as daddy reached into his pocket and took out his little black change purse. He scratched around in one side and handed the tall young boy two dimes.

"Thank you," said Buzzy as he turned to leave.

"Have some supper," said daddy.

"No thank you, I have a lot of stops to make before dark."

Buzzy was a seventeen-year-old high school senior and still delivering papers. He had been our paperboy since he took over the delivery from Jeanette Turner shortly before he was nine years old. We never thought that one so young would stick with such a grueling job, but he did. Eddie White owned the route and hired Buzzy to deliver the papers in lower Madison Heights for two dollars a week. Buzzy walked the entire route. Sometimes

An old change purse

"Buzzy" McBride delivering papers

A Cushman motor scooter

he would run the route, trying to see how far he could run each day. Later, he purchased the route from Eddie for 25 dollars. As he expanded his operation, he was able to purchase a bicycle.

He delivered the Lynchburg evening newspaper, the *Daily Advance*, Monday through Saturday. Customers paid 20 cents a week for the six newspapers. Buzzy paid the news office 12 cents and he kept eight. When other boys his age were trying to find a part-time job, he was faithfully working and developing his paper route that he had operated for the past eight years.

David Crews owned the paper route in upper Madison Heights beginning at Sixth Street. Later, when it became available Buzzy also bought that route for 25 dollars. He quickly learned it was too much for him to deliver so he hired Lawrence Cooper to work for him. They divided the route so that each of them had between 80 and 85 customers. When Buzzy was 14 he was able to buy a Cushman motor scooter to use to deliver his papers.

The newspapers were dropped off at Raymond Woody's store each afternoon, which was at the north end of Main Street. Buzzy and Lawrence delivered everything from the store to the top of Stump's Hill and halfway down Rocky Hill to "Shine" Cooper's house. Occasionally he would have a few papers left at the end of the day and would sometimes sell one to the Cooper's neighbor, Mr. Oscar Martin.

This young entrepreneur was an inspiration to the residents of our community. His pleasing personality, his work ethic, and his commitment to his customers would continue to serve him well in his chosen profession as an optician for more than five decades after he had given up his paper route.

Chapter 13

James Roland "Jimmie" Turner

As soon as I arrived home from school I hurried into the kitchen where mama was busy cooking supper. "I'm going to play some football," I said, grabbing a couple of cookies and pouring myself a glass of milk.

"Change clothes before you leave, you have to wear those to school tomorrow. Be back in time for supper, your daddy has some work for you to do."

"Yes ma'am," I said as I hurried off upstairs to change.

Some of the boys were already passing the ball when I arrived at Otis Doss's yard. The terraced area behind his house had once been leveled for a garden, but since he didn't plant it he allowed us to use it for a football field. It was too small for baseball, but was great for our football games. Soon there were enough guys there to start a game. About that time, Tommy (not his real name) rode up on his bike. I wondered how he had heard about the game since he didn't go to our school. He was a big kid and the only one that owned a helmet and shoulder pads. He wasn't fun to tackle, but we didn't let that stop us; we learned to hit him low.

The game started and Tommy returned the kick. He made it halfway up the field before we stopped him. We continued to batter each other around for about fifteen minutes as we carried the ball back and forth up the field. Jimmie Turner caught the kick and started up the field with the ball. The other team was all over him. When he dug himself out from under the pile of bodies he yelled, "Time out! I've got to put my leg back on." Everybody took a break while Jimmie reattached his artificial leg.

Jimmie's right leg had been amputated below the knee when he was about twelve years old as a result of a hunting accident. With youth on his side, he quickly recovered from the surgery and began to adapt to his modified lifestyle. He was soon speeding around on crutches and playing sports again. He would bat a ball standing on one leg and a crutch and then run to first on his crutches.

Artificial limbs were expensive and money was scarce. Our Boy Scout troop decided we would raise funds to help him purchase a prosthesis. I remember going door to door in the community and asking people for donations. Jimmie soon had his prosthesis. The picture below shows Jimmie before he received his artificial leg. After adapting to his new leg, he was unstoppable. He never allowed his handicap to keep him from participating in life to the fullest. Hunting, fishing, and sandlot baseball were pursued with vigor. Even the neighborhood tackle football games like the one described above were not off limits for him.

He instilled in his children the same love for sports that he had and they were always formidable opponents on the field. His love for his family, his community, his church, and God was a tremendous legacy he left behind when he died unexpectedly in 1999. He was the epitome of a person who learned to live a victorious life in spite of difficult circumstances. May his story challenge others to do likewise.

"JIMMIE" TURNER AND FRIENDS
Mrs. Brown's 6th Grade Class, 1948, Jimmie is second from left.
Left to right: Carrol Bryant, Jimmie Turner, Billy Ogen, Alfred Bryant, Ed Williams, Jean Bryant, Ann Rosser, Joan Hunt, and Joyce Hunt

Chapter 14

James Richard "Jimmie" Ray

If there had been an "Official Photographer of Madison Heights," James Richard "Jimmie" Ray (1910-1983) would have deserved the title. Not many special events took place without Jimmie being called upon to record them on film. I include some of his photos in this chapter, and you will also see them scattered throughout this book.

Much information on Jimmie Ray and his family was submitted to *Amherst County Virginia Heritage 1761-1999* (Walsworth Publishing Co) by Jimmie's nephew, Marshall Neil Baldwin. Jimmie was the youngest of seven children born to Marshall and "Mollie" Walton Ray. When Marshall died in 1915 at age 48, the four older children had to quit school and go to work to help provide for the family. The widowed mother sold cosmetic and toiletry items door-to-door and also taught private piano lessons. Three of the children, Lucas, James, and Mabel, never married and continued living at their home place with their mother until their death.

For most of these years, Lucas, a postal worker, was the principal breadwinner. Jimmie worked 14 years for the Craddock Terry shoe factory in Lynchburg before joining the U.S. Navy in 1943. After he was discharged from the Navy he became an employee of S.O. Fisher, a Lynchburg sporting goods store. About 1945 he started "Jimmie's Studio" in a little building in the back yard of his home on Main Street. He took photographs and provided photo finishing for the public and other commercial photographers until his death.

Scott's Mill

Jimmie Ray

Schools and churches in Madison Heights and the surrounding area sought his services frequently for special events. He was often present for weddings and other family affairs. Individuals also came to his studio for portraits. Jimmie's sister, Mabel, assisted him in the studio and in the days before color film, she tinted many of the final prints. The pictures in this chapter are samples of some of his work.

Many area residents have seen the picture of Scott's Mill built in 1883 by J.J. Scott and destroyed by fire about 1943. Eleanor Tankersly donated an enlarged copy of the picture to Aylor's Farm and Garden store at Forest and said her brother, "Garvin E. Tankersly took the picture when he was employed by S.O. Fisher." She says "she did not know who produced the enlargement." Jimmie Ray produced enlargements and his sister, Mabel, tinted them. Because I have owned an enlargement for over 40 years, I had assumed Jimmie took the picture. Perhaps it was a joint venture of Jimmie and Garvin since both of them once worked for S.O. Fisher. I

Jimmie's studio

Mabel Ray tinting picture of Scott's Mill

JIMMIE RAY'S FAMILY, 1947
Billy Ray's seventh birthday party.
Left to right, standing: Mrs. Howard (Bessie) Ray, Lucas Ray, Howard Ray, Elmo Baldwin, Mollie Ray, Neil Baldwin, Mabel Ray, Dolly Baldwin, Dorothy Baldwin. Two boys in center: Billy Ray and Kyle Baldwin.

willingly give credit to both of them for whatever part they had in preserving this historical building on film. The picture on the previous page shows Mabel Ray tinting an enlarged picture of Scott's Mill.

This seems to be an appropriate place to express my gratitude to some of Jimmie Ray's family members for their role in preserving his picture files for future generations and also making them available for me to use. Marshall Neil Baldwin and Ann Drumheller Baldwin are shown on the next page in their 1957 wedding picture. Neil, the oldest nephew, moved the bulk of Jimmie's files to his home to preserve them after Jimmie died. Following Neil's death, Ann has overseen the care of the pictures. Nephews Kyle Baldwin and Billy Ray are the only two family members shown in the photo above that are still alive. The four Goodman children shown on the next page are the children of Richard Goodman and Neil's deceased sister, Dorothy.

Ann, Kyle, Debbie and Rhonda have helped me locate many of the pictures used in this book and given me permission to use them. Without their help it would have been impossible for me to complete this pictorial record of Madison Heights. Thank you Ann, Kyle, Debbie and Rhonda! Four more family pictures are shown on the next page followed by nine more pictures of Jimmie's work.

SOME OF JIMMIE RAY'S FAMILY PICTURES

Neil and Ann 1957

The Goodman children: Lisa, Rhonda, Debbie & Mark, 1966

KYLE BALDWIN'S NINTH BIRTHDAY
Left to right, front: Gloria Martin, Billy Ray, Brenda Layne, Gay Coffey holding Jane Johnson, Gay Robertson, Judy Martin holding Thomas Martin, Shelby Farmer, and Jerry Walton. Back: Raleigh Campbell, Freddie Coffey, Neil Baldwin, Marilyn DeWitt, Kyle Baldwin and Dorothy Baldwin.

DOROTHY BALDWIN'S SIXTEENTH BIRTHDAY
Left to right, seated: Lois Goodman, Peggy Farmer, Mary Scott, Dallas Gillispie, Mary Jane Lang, Dorothy Baldwin, And Patsy Purdue. Standing: Richard Goodman, R.O. Woody, Donald Owen, James Morcom, Neil Baldwin, Shirley Campbell, Faye Gillispie And Barbara Ray

FOUR SIBLINGS
Viola Marks Stinson, Jack Marks, Roberta Marks Cash, Wiley Marks. 25th Wedding Anniversary of John A. "Jack" Marks and Mary R. Marks

1948 BIRTHDAY PARTY
Left to right, seated: Lemuel "Lem" Harrell, Wayne Dawson, unknown, Lawrence Dawson Jr., Shirley Woody, Dorothy "Dot" Harrell, Otis "Sonny" Doss Jr.
Standing: Lillian Shaner, Joann Crews, R.O. Woody, Lynn Woody, Neil Baldwin, Peggy Farmer, Connie Martin, Mildred Walton, Wade Rucker, Jean Shaner. (Permission by Lawrence Dawson, Jr.)

FOUR GENERATIONS
Left to right: Matt Marks Walker (Mrs. John), Hilda Walker Hawkins (Mrs. Leroy), Loretta Hawkins Foster (Mrs. John), and Cheryl (now Mrs. Charles Wynn) Permission by Loretta H. Foster

DELUXE CLEANERS GIRLS SOFTBALL TEAM
Left to right, Batboy: Clarence Shaner. Front row: Kathleen Walker, Jean Shaner, Lillian Shaner, Patsy Walker, Juanita Duff, Sylvia Walker, Nancy Woody. Back row: Phyllis Abbitt, Lois Tyree, Phyllis Tyree, Mae Martin, Dot Foster, Marie Wood, Louise Goolsby, Marie Abbitt, and Nancy Cash.

FIFTIETH WEDDING ANNIVERSARY
Tom and Nannie Carroll, seated. Left to right, back row: Nancy Carroll, Jesse Bell Carroll, Walter Carroll, Lacy Woody, Evelyn Carroll Woody, "Buddy" Woody, Joann Woody. Front row: Thomas Carroll Woody, Pamela Ann Woody (children of Buddy and Joann). Taken 1954 at the Timberlake home of Lacy and Evelyn Woody. Permission by Nancy Carroll and Joann Woody.

Tom and Nannie Carroll lived on the corner of Third and Main Street. Their yard was surrounded by a white picket fence, built and maintained by Tom. It also contained a unique glider-type swing that he built which was probably his own design. Nannie loved to raise chickens in a little lot hidden away in the back corner of the yard. She sold eggs and according to her granddaughter, Nancy Carroll, kept her egg money hidden under the tablecloth on her kitchen table.

ODD FELLOWS & REBECCAS BANQUET
January 26, 1950, Methodist Church Fellowship Hall
Although I know many of the people pictured on this page it is impossible to identify everyone in this large crowd. There were two more tables in the room to accommodate members and the invited guests.

TEEN TIME CLUB
Madison Heights High School auditorium, May 1950
Left to right, front: two unknown children. First row: Betty Gail Eggleston, Dorothy Baldwin, Lois Arthur, Jane Arnold, Patricia Perdue (Queen) Connie Martin (King), Ray Goff, James Camden, and Richard Goodman.
Second row: Faye Gillispie, Nancy Campbell, Joan Barker, Buzzy McBride, Frank Murphy, Jr., Lawrence Cooper, and James Story.
Third row: Mildred Walton, Tillie Terry, Phyllis Arthur, Sonny Banton, Richard Morcom, Thomas Manley, and Jimmy Morcom.
Fourth row: Marilyn Dewitt, Kitty Scott, Audrey Goff, Barbara Ray, Betty Crews, Gwen Clements, and Doris Patterson.

According to some of the surviving members, it seems that the primary purpose of this club was for teen fellowship and they received their adult leadership from Henry Neil Morcom. They usually met at the old Odd Fellows Hall on Fourth Street in Madison Heights, but on this special occasion they met at the high school.

GIBBS PIANO RECITAL - 1949
Left to right, seated in front row: Sylvia McCraw, Patsy Woodroof, Gay Coffee, and Patsy Bryant. Standing: J.T. Banton, unknown, Nancy Campbell, Donna Jean Thacker, unknown, Carolyn McIvor, Joyce Coffee, Doris Patterson, Copey Jones, Connie Gouyer, Marilyn Dewitt, Florence Foster, Barbara Knowles, Ollie Mae Stowe, Sandra McCraw, Jeanette Shaner seated at the end of the piano, Mrs. Olivia Gibbs seated at the piano, James Swisher, Gerry McCraw, James Story and Jimmie Goff.

If Jimmie Ray deserved the title of Official Photographer of Madison Heights than Mrs. Olivia Gibbs would probably deserve the title of "Official Piano Teacher of Madison Heights." It is impossible for me to know how many people took piano lessons from her, but the 24 students shown above was probably a normal sized group that she taught each year.

Mrs. Gibbs lived on Rt. 29 at the top of Madison Heights hill (new road hill) and taught students in her home. Her house was located on the bus line which made it convenient for most of the students to go directly from school for afternoon classes and then ride the bus home. More than half of the students pictured above lived on the bus line, but some lived at Monroe, Elon, and other places.

I am not sure of the frequency of the piano recitals, but I believe they were annual events and normally held at Madison Heights High School like the one above.

Chapter 15

Raymond Deal

The four men moved slowly up the flooded river in the small boat. They traveled just inches away from their neighbor's yards, calling out to residents in each house to assure they were safe and had no needs. The man in the bow watched anxiously for hidden obstacles under the surface of the water or large pieces of floating debris coming downstream. Raymond Deal stood in the stern tending the small engine that propelled them against the current. He looked up and smiled as one of his neighbors stepped from the house to take a picture.

1969 flood from Hurricane Camille

The two men in the center of the boat sat quietly watching the raging torrent they had seen too many times before. River Road lay many feet below the bottom of their boat, covered by the caramel water. Beyond the tree-lined riverbank the mighty James surged eastward, taking with it anything it could carry. Huge trees inched their way downstream towards Scott's Mill dam. Some of them would be

The record flood of 1985

swept over the dam while larger ones would come to rest against the stone structure where they would slowly deteriorate or wait for the next flood to carry them further downstream.

The men in the boat were no strangers to the James River at flood stage. While others came from outlying places just to gawk at the swollen stream, most of the River Road people would be fighting for survival until the water began to recede. When the river left its banks, many of the residents had to move to higher ground with their possessions where they were sometimes isolated. Property damage and loss were common. When the river eventually returned to its banks it left behind the formidable task of cleaning up mud.

Because of the nature of their community, the River Road residents possessed a lot of knowledge about the James River and a great deal of respect for it. Several generations of some families have lived along the river and many have learned to use the river as a means of producing income. Boats, docks, stores, fishing, camping, selling fish bait and catering to those who pursued these interests were some of the ways that produced income for the River Road people.

Raymond's father, James "Jim" Deal, Sr., was in poor health for many years and unable to work a regular job. He worked part-time at Bibee's Supermarket on the corner of Seventh and Main Streets in Lynchburg. He supplemented his income by other means when possible. He had the job of monitoring the daily river height and reporting it to the weather service at Lynchburg Municipal Airport (then called Preston Glenn Airport) during the 1940s. This was made possible by a drop cable stationed in a locked box on the west side of Williams Viaduct. Jim would measure the river height daily and phone it in to D.T. Jackson at the airport. "This is Jim

Deal," he would say, "reporting the river gage reading." During seasons of heavy rain or when the threat of a flood was imminent he would monitor it several times a day. Raymond says his dad "received 50 cents for each reading." He would usually call from Bibee's store or from Smiley's sand plant on the river. (More about that on the following pages.)

Jim Deal also supplemented his income by selling minnows. He would catch minnows and sell them to fishermen. When his health no longer allowed him to catch them, Raymond and his brothers, James and Garland, would catch them and their mom would sell them. Mr. Deal developed a unique way to keep his minnows. He used five-gallon lard cans to keep his minnows in. These metal cans had a press-on top and a fold-down handle on each side near the top. He used a nail and hammer to punch holes in the can so water could pass through it. The holes had to be punched from the inside out so there were no sharp edges inside to harm the minnows. The holes were punched from the top down to within three inches of the bottom. The minnows were placed in the can, a rope was tied to the handle, and the can submerged in the river. When he needed minnows, he retrieved the can, the water drained out of the holes leaving the minnows swimming around in three inches of water where they were easily scooped out and sold for 15 cents a dozen.

EIGHT GUYS FROM RIVER ROAD
Left to right: Bo Deal, Howard "Pee Wee" Proffitt, Junior Deal, Wes Robbins, Raymond Deal getting his ears pulled by Ike Floyd, and Clayton Proffitt standing in front of Junior Cyrus.

Dredging sand from James River

In the 1930s Jack Smiley found another way to produce income from the mighty James when he established a sand plant on its bank and began to dredge sand from the river bottom. The operation was located above Scott's Mill dam for most of its nearly 50 years of existence.

A dredge boat would pump the sand onto a barge to be unloaded by a crane onshore. The sand was delivered to customers by Smiley dump trucks or commercial haulers. When sand became scarce, the plant was relocated up river above Reusens. The pumping operation required one to three men, depending on the type system being used, and up to three support men on shore. The sand plant was later owned by Concrete Ready Mix of Lynchburg who was selling about 10,000 cubic yards of sand each year. The operation was forced to close by the Environmental Protection Agency in 1979. It was not closed because of the damage being done by pumping the sand out, but because they were discharging trash back into the river. The pump picked up cans, bottles, shoes, and other trash which was screened out of the sand and fell back into the water. That was illegal. They could take it out, but they couldn't put it back in!

This March 1962 photo shows the three vessels used for the three-man operation, the tugboat on the left, the barge in the center, and the dredge boat behind the barge extending out to the right side. Operators in this picture are Raymond Deal, Manson "Red" Proffitt, and Walter Davis. Raymond, who was known to his co-workers by the nickname of "Joe," normally worked as the dispatcher when this picture was taken. He apparently was substituting for Carrington "Tody" Proffitt who was the regular barge worker for many years.

Raymond Deal and the dredge boat

The dredge boat was all metal while the barge was all wood. The barge had gates on each end plus four or five gates spaced at intervals throughout the boat dividing it into compartments. It would hold 20 or more cubic yards of sand, which weighed 2500 lbs per yard. If sand were plentiful in the area being pumped the barge could be loaded in ten minutes. The dredge boat was left anchored in the river unless it had to be brought in for maintenance or there was danger of a flood. The tugboat transported the two barges back and forth to shore, replacing the full barge with an empty one. The tugboat operator also used metal-tipped push poles to move the barge side to side during the loading operation to equalize the weight. The tug boat was operated by many different people during the 1950s and 1960s.

Later, the operation was modified so it could be conducted with only one man. For many years Raymond "Joe" Deal was that man. Raymond's father died young after being in ill health for many years and the 15 year-old-boy went to work at the sand plant in 1947 to help support his family. He worked there until it closed 32 years later. He says, "When I started working there I was making $16 dollars a week, forty cents an hour for a forty hour week."

In the early 1940s, Rev. Gordon Ingram organized a mission church on River Road a short distance above Scott' Mill Dam. The church was called Riverside Mission and services were held on Sunday afternoon at three and Thursday evenings at eight. Raymond Deal and his family attended this church. The picture below was taken in the summer of 1942.

THE RIVERSIDE MISSION
Left to right: Patsy Ingram, Gordon Ingram Jr., James Deal in front of Gladys Freeman, Margie Freeman, Ethel Scott behind Betty Lou Bibb, Clayton Proffitt in front of Inez Proffitt (L) and Helen Proffitt, Raymond Deal in front of Jean Bibb and Mrs. Holt, Dewey Proffitt, Howard Proffitt in front of Lois Freeman and Mrs. Branch (with hat in last row) and Loraine Freeman on her left, Evelyn Proffitt in front of Rena Freeman (with hat in second row), and Arlene Ingram, unknown girl in front of Mrs. Draper (also has hat in second row), and Jesse Deal and Addie Deal, unknown woman, (in front row with Bible under arm) in front of Beatrice Proffitt. Last girl on right is Peggy Bibb standing in front of Mrs. Litchford and Sara Smith. Man in right rear is Clark Freeman holding granddaughter, Phyllis Scott. Man in back row on left with hat is the pastor, Gordon Ingram. (Thanks to Elizabeth Freeman for identifying the people in this picture.)

Chapter 16

Willie "Sweetie" Hughes, The River Man

I was seven years old when we received news that Sweetie Hughes had drowned. Everyone was shocked. If it had been anyone else in the community the surprise would not have been as great, but Sweetie Hughes? Nobody knew the river as well as Sweetie. Although he was only fifty years old, he was a local legend. When someone drowned in the James River people would say, "Call Sweetie, he'll find them. He knows that river like the palm of his hand." I have not been able to locate anyone today who can remember the exact number of bodies he recovered from the river, but some think it was more than ten. Now the river had claimed Sweetie as its latest victim.

Sweetie lived on Stumps Hill with his wife, Maude, and their children in the first house on the right as you went up the hill. A couple of the older children were married, but the youngest, Emmett, was 12 when his daddy died. He vividly remembers the mid-March 1942 event and becomes somber when talking about

"Sweetie" Hughes and John Henry Tyree, two friends on a fishing trip.

River dragging operation, Lynchburg Life Saving Crew

it. He remembers the two-day dragging operation conducted by the Lynchburg Life Saving Crew that yielded no results. The search was similar to one conducted a few years earlier for a boy that had drowned near William's Viaduct. Emmett remembers that the boy's mother sat on the bank weeping as the crew searched unsuccessfully for his body. Sweetie asked the mother to show him where the boy had disappeared in the water and she did. According to Emmett, Sweetie drove a nail in the end of the boat pole, bent it over and began probing the river bottom from his boat. He soon located the boy's body and pulled it to the surface. Now Sweetie's body was in the water and needed locating. Who would come forward to find him?

Sweetie and some of his friends had been net fishing at night below the Ninth Street falls near the Lynchburg shore when their boat capsized. His son-in-law, who could not swim, clung to the boat with two other passengers while Sweetie swam for help. All of the men felt confident he would make it even though the melting of a late-season snow had pushed the river towards flood stage. Although he was a good swimmer, he was ill equipped for the occasion, wearing heavy boots that quickly filled with the frigid water. Family members also remember that he had recently suffered from serious cramps in his arms. Apparently the combination was too great for him, since he never reached the shore.

Emmett Hughes

Harry Hughes, Sweetie's oldest son, worked on the railroad. He was working nearby when he heard cries for help coming from the river. He phoned the Lynchburg Life Saving Crew who responded and rescued the men from the water. It wasn't until later that they discovered that Sweetie had never made it to shore.

Billy, another one of Sweetie's sons, worked at Glamorgan Pipe and Foundry. As the search operation continued without results, he and Harry became determined to locate their Dad. Billy went to Glamorgan and made a metal hook to fit on the end of the boat pole, but thought the trauma would be more than he could stand if he found him. Harry took charge and soon located his father's body. When he pulled him to the surface he became so distraught that he released him. A nearby Life Saving Crew dragging team responded to his calls and recovered the body.

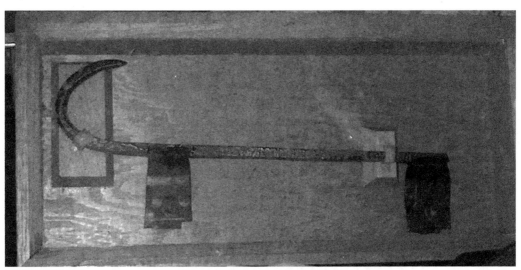
METAL HOOK
This hook was used to locate the body of "Sweetie" Hughes

CHAPTER 17

Clayton Wright,
The Indescribable One

How can I describe Clayton Wright? It would be simpler to leave this chapter out, and one of Clayton's friends advised me to do that, but no book about Madison Heights would be complete without a story about Clayton. Although he has already appeared in the picture of the 1948 Madison Heights High School championship baseball team, baseball is hardly his claim to fame (unless he has acquired an unreported fortune betting on the professional teams).

I suppose the question that begs to be asked is "What is his claim to fame?" Third generation storekeeper, brick salesman, entrepreneur, campground operator, restauranteur, or

Clayton Wright, four-and-a-half-months old on the front porch of his home. J.M. Wright's store is shown in background.

THE WRIGHT FAMILY
Front: Raleigh. Back: left to right, Aubrey, Lois, and Clayton

funeral home associate are all possible answers, but none of these alone communicates the essence of Clayton Wright. I realized as I struggled with this description that his various vocations do not define who he is. He brought his own definition to each vocation.

I've known Clayton all my life. We lived about two blocks from each other and attended school together. He's not going to like me telling that he is much older than I am, but I'm delighted to share that he graduated from school four years before I did. I know what his rebuttal will be: "Charles was so dumb that it took him that much longer to get through school." He may even come up with one better than that. Regardless of what he says, neither of us failed a year. I worked hard and passed, he charmed the teachers and passed.

In addition to seeing him at school, I saw Clayton often at Wright's Store, the family store founded by his grandfather "Jim" Wright, and operated in our time by his father, Aubrey. It was the closest store to my house and a favorite hangout for young and old alike. It was even better if you had a nickel for a Pepsi or an RC Cola. By the time I was old enough to trudge to the store, Clayton was already working there. He'll probably tell you he ran it single-handedly from the time he was six years old. If you have any doubts (I know some will), you can ask his 97-year-old mother, Lois, who is still living at the time of this writing.

When I was trying to locate some pictures of Wright's store in its heyday I called Clayton. After a long delay he picked the phone up and said, "C-h-a-r-l-e-s!"

I said, "You were looking at the caller ID before you answered weren't you? You probably wouldn't have answered if you hadn't been curious about why I'm calling."

"I always talk to preachers," he said.

"I'm writing a book about Madison Heights and I'm putting a chapter in it about you."

"Good!"

"I'm having a problem writing it. I've worn my dictionary out trying to find words to describe you."

"Perfect," he said. "Perfect, is the only word you need!"

After we finished bantering, we talked some about the good old days in Madison Heights and lamented the changes. Clayton is at his best when he is swapping insults with his friends and everybody he meets is his friend.

Many people have eaten a Mallo Cup. These delicious little chocolate, coconut, and marshmallow cream filled cups still come with a game card inside. Once they had a promotion game where the cards each had a letter printed on them. When you collected enough to spell Mallo Cup you could mail them in and receive 12 free candies. There was only one catch; all the letters were plentiful except the M. I walked into Wright's Store one day, put a nickel on the counter and told Clayton, "I want a Mallo Cup."

"I guess you want an M," he taunted.

"Yep," I said.

"Here's one," he said, pitching the candy on the counter. I picked it up and ripped

INSIDE WRIGHT'S STORE
Lois Wright waiting on Minnie Dawson (left)

CLAYTON WRIGHT AND HIS COUSINS
Left to right, front: Jerome Cooper and Charles Layne. Rear: Clayton Wright, Shirley Wright, Carlton Layne, Lawrence Cooper, and Kenneth Layne

the paper off. It was an M.

Wright's Store offered both credit and delivery to its customers. In my time they had a delivery truck and some of the high school boys drove it. Clayton or his cousins Carlton Layne or his brother Kenneth usually drove the truck. When the weather was nice it was fun for us to ride along in the back of the truck on the delivery runs. We paid for our ride by hopping off at each stop and delivering the groceries.

According to Clayton, the credit system was a bit more complex than the delivery and was often expanded to cover more than groceries. He said the laundry man, who picked up and delivered laundry to your home each week, would sometimes stop by the store and say, "Mrs. Smith wasn't home so I need to leave her laundry here." Aubrey would take the laundry, pay the bill and add it to the family's ticket at the store.

Even the county taxman got in on the act. Mr. Drummond, our tax collector, would mail a "penny postcard" to everyone in lower Madison Heights telling him or her he would be at Wright's Store on a certain day to collect taxes. On the day he was scheduled to come, Aubrey would tell his wife, "Lois, fix a nice lunch today, Mr. Drummond will be here to eat." People would walk to the store and pay their taxes in cash. Checking accounts were unheard of in those days. Clayton said that occasionally someone would call his dad and say, "I can't get to the store today to pay my taxes, will you pay them for me and add it to my account?"

Like every community, we had our share of interesting people who hung out at the store. Craig Rucker was a reclusive older man who lived alone in the basement of the Odd Fellows Hall one-half a block away. Craig was usually unkempt and walked poorly in high top shoes that loosely fitted his sockless feet. He used a cane for assistance when he walked to the store. If the weather was nice he would sometimes sit for hours on the steps outside the store. He was difficult to talk to and most people didn't try, they simply spoke to him and continued on. When the weather was bad and he didn't show up at he store, Aubrey would usually send Clayton or someone else to check on him to be sure he was still alive and see if he needed anything. There were so many stories that circulated about Craig that it was difficult for me to separate truth from fiction. I do know that his family once owned a beautiful home perched high on the river bluff where I.H. McBride Sign Company is now located. Old pictures taken from Lynchburg show the huge house located on "Rucker's Hill" before it was destroyed by fire.

Some of the patients from the Colony had freedom to visit our community and some worked odd jobs for people. Sometimes after they had earned money they would be afraid to take it back to the Colony so they would put it in a little cloth tobacco bag and get Aubrey to keep it for them in the store safe. The bags of tobacco were used for rolling cigarettes. You could buy a bag with a package of cigarette papers attached for a nickel. That was the most economical way to smoke, but few people could roll nice cigarettes.

The second most economical way was Marvel cigarettes, which cost 12 cents a pack when most other brands were 18 cents. Aubrey Wright kept an open pack of Marvels on the cash register and sold them loose for one cent each. I suspect many boys began their smoking career with these penny cigarettes since there was no age restriction on buying them.

One of the best-known Colony patients was Frisco, an older man who came to town almost every Saturday. Most everybody in the community knew him. Charles Irvin mentions him in *Amherst County Virginia Heritage Volume II*, (Walsworth Publishing Co. 2004) and adds "he always wore about a dozen neck ties around his neck and was headed to Lynchburg to the movie."

In the 1960s when both Clayton and I had moved from "Old Town" Madison Heights to Seminole Drive, he called me one night. "Charles, this is Clayton. Robert says that you're getting ready to build a new house."

"I am."

"Good! I want to sell you the bricks for it."

"I'm don't think I'm going to build a brick house."

"What are you going to build?"

"A rock house."

Clayton and his daughter Rebecca, taken at the wedding of Rebecca and Eric Hughes, 1996

"You should be able to shake your head and get enough rocks for that!"

"If I can't I'll call you and you can give me a few of yours."

"If you change your mind, let me know."

"If I change my mind, I'll probably use old brick. I like the way they look."

"You don't want to do that! You'll regret it if you do. They look nice for a while, but those old bricks are porous. They soak up water and freeze and crumble. I can take you and show you some. Let me come by and show you and Irene some samples of our bricks that look like old bricks. They are wood molded seconds. They have color variations, are irregular, and if you mix a few black and white ones in them they look just like old brick, but they don't crumble."

I built my new brick house in 1963 just the way Clayton suggested and bought the bricks from him. When we got ready to build again in 1980, Clayton was no longer selling bricks. Because we liked the bricks so well on our first house we also used them on our second house and bought them from the same company. I didn't tell Clayton about it; I was afraid he would want a commission.

Chapter 18

Harry Walton the Barber

Three boys sat on the bench listening to the conversations taking place between Harry Walton, the barber, and the customers who had gathered that evening. It was a fun place to hang out if the weather was bad or if there was nothing else to do. If you needed a haircut it usually wasn't hard to get one or more of your buddies to tag along with you. Occasionally a woman would bring her little boy in for a haircut, but usually it was an all-male gathering where the conversations would often become risqué, much to the delight of the boys. At the end of the evening they were well equipped with stories to share with their friends the next day.

Harry was cutting Homer Tyree's hair when Elmo Baldwin and Jimmie Ray walked in. Jimmie had his camera.

"I think I'd better leave," said Homer to the barber. "It looks like you're getting ready to have a family reunion here tonight and I'm not a family member."

"We'll let you stay," said Elmo, "if you promise to behave."

"I'm not making any promises until I find out what Jimmie's gonna do with that camera."

"I'm wondering about that too," chuckled Harry.

"Everybody's afraid of my camera," said Jimmie. "Elmo said he was coming down for a haircut so I decided to trudge along and take a picture of my legendary cousin cutting my brother-in-law's hair."

THREE BOYS ON A BENCH
Left to right: Robert Stinson, Kenneth Layne and Reggie Arthur

"Aren't you afraid of what that might do to your camera?" laughed Homer.

"I thought about that, but I came up with a solution. I'll take your picture first. If that doesn't break it, I'll take theirs."

The three boys were enjoying the bantering as they watched Jimmie prepare his camera for action. Turning towards them he said, "Let me practice with you boys. Slide over close to each other and act like you're friends."

After taking their picture he turned to Homer. "I may as well take yours too before I break it on the other two." Homer cut his eyes towards Jimmie and said, "Mr. Walton, if I had known all of this was going to happen, I would have stayed home tonight. If he sends me a bill for this picture I'm going to send it to you!"

Walton's Barber Shop was strategically located at the intersection of Main Street and the Colony Road in the corner of the yard of the old Walton home where two of Harry's siblings still lived. The Walton's cousins, Jimmie, Lucas, and Mabel Ray, lived immediately behind the small barbershop in the Ray home place.

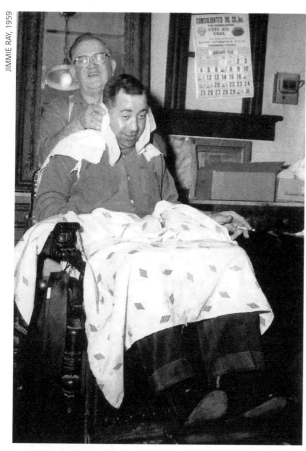

Harry Cutting Homer Tyree's hair

Harry loved to tease the young boys when he cut their hair. When he finished, he would take some sweet smelling tonic, rub it between his hands and dampen their hair before he combed it. He always told the boys he was putting "a little skunk pee" on their hair.

Harry Walton's Barber Shop was one of two in Madison Heights. Emmett Coffee operated the other one, which was located less than a block away. Both of the men were part-time barbers with flexible evening schedules. In a recent discussion with Robert "Bobby" Bell, we were discussing what Harry charged for a haircut. I was thinking he charged 35 cents, later increasing it to 50 cents. Bobby thinks it began at 25 cents for children and varied depending on the type of haircut you received. If you wanted to leave your sideburns, the extra trimming and shaving cost more. He also remembers the old manual clippers that Harry used and how they would pull your hair if they weren't sharp.

Usually when we needed a haircut we would walk up the road to see if either shop was open. Although some customers had a preference, they usually settled for the one that was open or the least crowded. Time was also a consideration for some

The Ray family home

Walton's Barber Shop

Harry Walton and his ornate barber chair

since Harry was a slower and more talkative barber. One "old-timer" remembers that sometimes a man who didn't want to wait would pay one of the boys who was waiting to let him take his place. Maybe that's why the boys hung around there in the evenings? Both men were good barbers. I regret that I don't have pictures of Emmett Coffey or his barbershop.

CHAPTER 19

John Holley, Jr. and a World War II Story

On July 7, 1959 I was drafted into the Army and sent to Fort Jackson, S.C. After Basic Training, I was reassigned there to attend Communications School. Following a two-week furlough, I drove my car when I returned to Fort Jackson. While I was attending school, I would drive home on free weekends.

I was returning to Fort Jackson one Sunday evening and stopped for gas at a little store in North Carolina. We didn't know what self-service gas was in those days. When you pulled up to a pump and stopped, somebody would come out and pump your gas. A man came from the store and said "How much?"

"Fill it up," I said.

"You from Madison Heights?" he asked.

Puzzled by the question, I turned to see him looking at my license plate. The Ruritan Club had sold Madison Heights strips as a fund-raiser. They were made to attach to a regular license plate and I had bought one and put it on my car. He was looking at that plate.

"Yeah, I'm from Madison Heights."

"You know John Holley?"

"I know two John Holleys. John Senior and John Junior."

"John Junior is the one I know. I was in the Army with him during World War

John Holley, Jr.

Two. We trained together, went overseas together, went through that ole war together and came back together. When you see him again tell him Harrison from North Carolina said hello."

"I will. I'll probably go home next weekend, I'll give him a call and tell him I saw you."

He finished pumping the gas, hung up the nozzle and turned around to face me again. "You want to hear something that happened to us that's hard to believe?"

"Sure."

"You know how the Army always organizes you in alphabetical order by your last name for everything you do?"

"Yeah, they still do that."

"There were three of us whose name started with the letter H: Harrison, Holley and Hunt. We trained at Fort Wheeler, Georgia. When they got ready to ship us overseas, they put us on a troop train to go cross-country because we were going to the Pacific. All three of us were in the same car. Each berth had a top, middle and lower bunk. Of course the lower bunk is the best and everybody wanted that. We decided to flip a coin to see who got it. Somebody said, 'Whoever gets the top bunk can have the bottom one when we come home.' I got the top bunk and rode it all the way to California where we shipped overseas to the war zone. We went through battle after battle, Guadalcanal, Philippines, and none of the three of us were killed. We shipped back to California after the War ended. When they put us on a troop train to come home, all three of us were assigned to one car again with three bunks to a berth. I walked in and pitched my stuff on the bottom bunk and said, 'O.K. boys, you can have the other two, this one is mine.'"

As I continued my trip to Fort Jackson, I thought about the story I had heard and wondered if it were true. If it were, what would be the odds of that happening? The next weekend when I returned home I called John, Jr. and told him I had met his old friend. He was elated. When I recited the story to him that Harrison had told me he said, "That's the truth. It was he, Garland Hunt, and I. It happened exactly like he told you."

Chapter 20

Movers and Shakers

Every organization knows the value of having good leadership to accomplish its goals. But what do you do in a small community that has no official organization? No mayor, town council or elected officers. As noted earlier, Madison Heights was dependent on Lynchburg for most services and Amherst County for some elected leadership. How did they meet other community needs? Volunteers were the answer. Where do you find volunteers? Primarily the church, the largest volunteer organization in the world. The second place would be civic and fraternal organizations. When things needed to be done in our community, the people knew who to contact to make it happen. In this chapter you see pictures of volunteers in action.

It is noteworthy that Mr. Ricketts was a Methodist, Miss Banton, an Episcopalian, and Mr. Freeman, a Baptist. I wish I knew the purpose of their meeting, but I don't. I can only assure you it was not an ecumenical meeting. It probably concerned installing streetlights, helping some needy family, or some other community project. They were likely selected as representatives from their churches. Miss Banton was the unofficial historian of Madison Heights, but was also active in every effort to better our community.

There were many other movers and shakers in our town, but no list would be complete without including Mrs. Vera Farmer Bryant. "Aunt Vera," as she was known

Bob Ricketts, Bertha Banton, and Walker Freeman

Lawrence Blanks Jr. and Vera Bryant

POPPY GIRLS, 1948
Left to right, first row: Linda Viar, Dottie Loving, Joanne Clements, Martha Lee Farmer, Barbara Viar, Gay Coffey, Shelby Farmer. Second row: Joan Barker, Betty Eggleston, Doris Patterson, Marilyn DeWitt, Linwood Wright. Third row: Patsy Perdue, Barbara Ray, Mildred Walton, Kathleen Walker, Dorothy Baldwin, Carolyn Spivey. Fourth row: Julia Manley, Tillie Terry, Kitty Scott, Mrs. Vera Bryant, Mary Brightwell and Shirley Cooper.

by many people, had the gift of getting things done. If a family had a house fire and needed furnishings, clothes, or even a house, she was the person to see. Active in Madison Heights Baptist Church and many civic organizations, she knew everybody in the area, knew their capabilities, and was gifted at getting people to use their resources for the good of the community.

Although I don't know Aunt Vera's role in the funding and construction of the memorial in the previous picture, it must have been significant for her to be involved in this dedication service in 1963. The plaque reads: "TO ALL THOSE OF MADISON HEIGHTS WHO GAVE THEIR LIVES IN THE ARMED SERVICES OF OUR COUNTRY. ERECTED BY A GRATEFUL COMMUNITY."

CHRISTMAS BASKET COMMITTEE, 1950
Left to right, front: Lewis Miller, Bertha Banton. Second row: Elmo Baldwin, unknown, Virginia Wood, Otis Doss, unknown, "Rink" Perdue, unknown. Third row: unknown, James Hughes, Freddie Viar, Rev. F.O. Briggs Rear: Hugh Wilson and Clark Mays.

Mrs. Vera Bryant was also involved in organizing the "Poppy Day" sales that were sponsored each Memorial Day weekend by the American Legion Auxiliary. She would recruit the children in the community to visit door-to-door collecting funds. The volunteers would distribute the little paper poppy flowers and receive donations for them. The funds were divided between the Disabled American Veterans organization and the Veterans Hospital at Salem, Virginia.

Collecting and distributing baskets of food and other items to needy families at Christmas was an annual event supported by the churches and civic organizations of our community. Pictured above, is a 15-member planning committee formed by representatives from these groups.

Chapter 21

The Last of the Peddlers

I feel privileged to have grown up in a community that had peddlers. Farmers would travel from their distant farms to sell their garden vegetables and other wares in the Madison Heights community. Three of these farmers used a horse and wagon to peddle their farm products. One of the men, Mr. Charlie Rakes, lived on Wright Shop Road near William's Run creek.

Another peddler, Mr. Bibb Ewers, also operated a farm on Wright Shop Road. The third peddler who used a horse and wagon was Mr. Watts who lived on Dixie Airport Road. He is the one I remember best because he came to our neighborhood more frequently than the others. The children loved to see him coming because we would hang on the back of the wagon and ride for several blocks. He would always say, "Now boys don't hang on the wagon, you might get hurt." We would stand there like little angels until he started driving away and then we would run catch him and hook our arms over the rear of the wagon and hang on. He could have benefited greatly from a rearview mirror. I think he knew we were there, but he never looked back.

While today's children seemingly receive no joy from visiting a giant supermarket with unlimited selections of food from around the world, it was a treat for us to greet the peddlers and hopefully sample some of their simple wares. I'm glad I was able to experience it.

Not all peddlers used horses. Bernice "Wheat" Ray used a truck to peddle produce. His early training with his father at Ray's Fruit and Produce in Lynchburg served him

Charlie Rakes and his horse Prince

"Wheat" Ray and his daughter Barbara

well after he was seriously injured on his job at the N&W Railroad. Unable to resume that railroad job, he became a produce broker working with local farmers, orchard men, and Canada Produce in Lynchburg. His peddling was primarily to local stores, but he also sold to individuals.

Terry Ray, the middle son in the family, remembers when orchard owners from Nelson and Amherst counties would contact his father about purchasing surplus apples from them. They would often deliver them to Madison Heights in the evening and load them onto his father's truck.

Canada Produce was one of the largest wholesale produce distributors in the area. Wheat Ray had a working relationship with them that provided him a yearlong supplier.

"Danny" Ray on his fathers truck, 1947
"Wheat" Ray's two-ton White heavy-duty truck loaded with apples.

Canada produce tractor trailers

Chapter 22

"Dumpsey's"

One of my weekly highlights following the scout meeting on Monday night at the Baptist church was to be able to buy a hot dog at Dumpsey's. Remember Mr. Johnny Hesson in Chapter Ten? His son, "Little Johnny" Hesson married Dumpsey Banton. Johnny had made a career of the U.S. Navy and returned to Madison Heights after he retired. He and Dumpsey opened a tiny little café on the corner of Seventh and Main Street across from her parents and sold hot dogs, snacks, and drinks. They didn't just sell hot dogs, they sold the "best hot dog" in the world featuring Dumpsey's homemade coleslaw. I loved them!

The picture below shows some of the assorted drinks, snacks, and smokes that were available to the customers. By today's standards they probably appear sparse, but not to us.

"Dumpsey" Banton Hesson

SIX FRIENDS AT DUMPSEY'S
Left to right, front: George T. Farmer, Lawrence Dawson Jr., and Otis "Sonny" Doss. Rear: Loy Banton, Jimmy Morcom, and Jimmy Davis. (about 1950)

During the 1940s (and possibly earlier) this building had been known as The Domino Inn. The older men in the community would gather there to play dominos. When the weather was nice they would sit outside on the sidewalk and play. When Dumpsey's opened, the older generation was immediately displaced by the young people. The building was too small to have tables, booths, or chairs, but that didn't matter. If you had food and friends, what more could you ask for?

One of the nice things about Dumpsey's was its central location in Old Town Madison Heights which made it within easy walking distance for everyone. The group in the picture below all lived within five blocks of the café. If you had a bike, it was only a short ride from home and you could be assured that you would find some of your friends there to hang out with. It was a great way to spend an evening.

Our community was grief-stricken when the news circulated one day that Johnny had "dropped dead" in his home from an apparent heart attack. Not only did we lose a good friend, but we lost something else that was important to the young people of our community. The little café we all loved never opened again.

"Little Johnny" Hesson standing outside of Dumpsey's, the Café operated by him and his wife

CHAPTER 23

The Mighty W.T.

A trip through Madison Heights today on U.S. 29 will take you past a 90-foot tall water tank located near the intersection of Lyttleton Lane. You may want to stop across the highway at McDonalds or Dairy Queen so you can get a better look at it. August 18, 1936 was the day of dedication for this 250,000-gallon monster that stored water for the Madison Heights community. Although I have no details of the dedication service, the following picture shows some of the local people who participated in the historic event.

According to Dan French, Director of Amherst County Service Authority, the city of Lynchburg owned the tank from 1936 until 1953 and Madison Heights purchased water from them. As the area grew, so did the need for more water. Lynchburg was unable to meet the need for an increased amount of water so Madison Heights built its own water filtration plant on Elon Road in 1953 and purchased the water tank from the city. The huge riveted steel structure was in need of maintenance and painting, which it received at the time of purchase. Besides storing water for the area, the high tank also is topped by a National Weather System antenna as a service to the community.

When the water tank was built in 1936, the area surrounding it was considered country. The streets near the water tank today did not exist and nearby Seminole Drive was only a gravel road. One of the first buildings erected in the area was a large frame structure that housed a café, grocery store, an apartment, and more. It was

DEDICATION SERVICE OF THE WATER TANK, AUGUST 18, 1936
Left to right, Margie Abbott, Vivian Miller, Gwendolyn Wood, James M. Wright, Margaret Holt, Marion Shaner and Odessa Holley.

THE WATER TANK CAFÉ
The Neon sign out front says "Bob Panel's Famous Mighty W.T. Café." Bob Panel was the owner when this picture was taken october 9, 1948. Notice how close it sits to the three lanes of Route 29.

ARMY CONVOY IN FRONT OF THE WATER TANK
Sunday, December 7, 1941, late afternoon

located on the edge of the busy highway only a few hundred yards from the water tank. It was aptly named "The Mighty W.T." which can be seen on the neon sign on the roof in the previous picture. Locals simply called it "The Water Tank."

The date of this convoy movement is significant: the day Pearl Harbor was bombed. I can't help but wonder if it wasn't coincidental that this large convoy (another picture shows many more vehicles) was already on the move that day. It's hard to believe they had been activated and were moving the same day because of the attack on Pearl Harbor. I chose to include this picture because it gives a good perspective of the highway, the café, and the water tank.

During its brief lifetime (roughly five years before and ten years after World War II), The Water Tank Café saw people from every level of life enter its doors, especially during the war years. Some of the stories I've heard aren't suitable for inclusion in this book, but others will give an idea of what life was like at The Water Tank Café.

When I asked one senior citizen about his experiences there he said, "I used to buy bootleg gas there during the war."

"What do you mean, bootleg?"

"I could buy it without stamps. Gas was rationed and we had to have ration stamps to buy it. I could buy it there without stamps for 25 cents a gallon."

"What did it cost with stamps?"

"I don't remember, but it must have been cheaper."

Inside the Water Tank Café, 1948

"Would you like to have some gas now for 25 cents a gallon?"

"All I could get!"

Many travelers stopped at The Water Tank because Route 29 was the major north-south highway through the area. It wasn't uncommon to encounter strangers there. One of my now-deceased relatives told me a story many years ago about an experience he once had there. He was a young man with his first car and was showing off by sliding around in the gravels in the parking lot. A stranger was watching him. After he parked, the stranger approached and began asking him questions about his car. Then the stranger asked him if he'd like to make 20 dollars. With nickel drinks and 25 cent gas, 20 dollars was a lot of money. That question was a no-brainer; sure he'd like to make 20 dollars. The man gave him specific directions about what he wanted him to do and the young man agreed to it.

On a certain evening at a specified time he was to go to a location in rural Amherst County, park his car, take a walk to a certain location, stay gone an exact amount of time, and return. He did as instructed and found his car loaded with cases of quart jars of moonshine whiskey. He was to deliver it to Lynchburg in an isolated area under Williams Viaduct near the Lynchburg Diamond Ice Factory. Again, he was to park, take a walk up town, stay a specified time and return. He did. The whiskey was gone and a twenty-dollar bill was in the front seat with a rock on it.

What a learning experience that was for the young man. While he was returning to Lynchburg with the load of whiskey he realized how stupid he was. He was hauling bootleg liquor for somebody and had no idea who it was. If he were caught, he would be the one sent to prison and the others would be free. He was taking that kind of risk for 20 dollars and wasn't even sure he would collect. Suppose he didn't get the money; what could he do about it? By the time he reached Lynchburg with the load of whiskey, he was scared stiff from fear. After the ordeal was over he realized he had never seen a person at the pick-up or delivery points. His only contact was a stranger he had never seen before, could not identify, and would never see again. He made 20 dollars that night, but he never had the desire to do it again.

The Water Tank Café was located less than five minutes from Madison Heights High School. In the early 1950s when one of my friends had a car at school we would often make a dash to The Water Tank for lunch. Hot dogs were two for a quarter and drinks were a nickel. Several people managed the café during its existence, but Aubrey Lee operated it during my high school years and continued until it was demolished a few years later because of highway construction. Keep in mind that this was no job for a sissy. All kinds of people walked through those doors and all kinds of situations arose. You had to be tough to run a café beside a busy highway. I remember a high school lunch break there in 1952. A hitchhiker came in (as they often did) and asked Aubrey how much a hot dog and a cup of coffee was.

"Hot dog is fifteen, coffee's a nickel," said Aubrey.

"I'll take a hot dog with everything on it," said the man, "and a cup of coffee." He sat down at the counter to wait.

Aubrey brought the traveler his food. He devoured the hot dog like he was starving and sat there sipping his coffee. I felt sorry for him and wondered what his story was. He stood to go and pulled exactly twenty cents from his pocket and handed it to Aubrey.

"Take it on up the road with you," said Aubrey. "That one's on me."

The man stared at him a moment in disbelief and said, "Thank you." He walked through the door and continued his journey north on Route 29. I had never seen that side of Aubrey Lee before. He was tough, but compassionate. I was proud of him and proud that he was one of us.

The water tank still stands like a faithful sentinel after 72 years of continuous service. The Water Tank Café has been gone for over 50 years. Most of the people who worked there are dead. The dangerous three-lane road has been replaced with a safer four-lane highway. The flow of traffic that reached its peak by the turn of the century has been significantly decreased by a new bypass. Fast food restaurants and other chain eateries line the highway where the cafes and Mom and Pop restaurants used to be. Shopping centers, a library, and a fire and rescue station are all within sight of the old tank. The water tank alone is deserving of the name it once was forced to share with others. It is indeed, "The Mighty W.T." If only it could talk.

PART FOUR:
My Gang

Chapter 24

Boy Scout Troop 33

Frank, my oldest brother, and Robert, my brother who was two years older than me, both belonged to Boy Scout troops in Lynchburg because we did not have one in Madison Heights. About 1947 the Methodist Church attempted to organize a troop and my brother, Earl, served for a short time as Scoutmaster. When changing circumstances forced Earl to give up his position, the troop failed because there was nobody else to assume leadership. It was difficult to obtain adult help at that time. Although I was too young to join the troop, I was anxious to join and had already learned all my requirements for Tenderfoot Scout. I was disappointed when the troop folded.

A few years later, the Baptist Church made another attempt to organize a troop and I was one of the first to join. I joined the troop and passed my Tenderfoot requirements the same night. I was rolling! The troop was blessed to have good leadership from the beginning. James Hughes, Hugh Wilson, Frank Lang, and Bill Pearce were all World War Two veterans and were committed to helping us boys become a first-class troop. Frank Lang, an ex-marine drill instructor, even taught us dismounted drills and made sure we knew how to "fall in" and "march!"

I've called this section MY GANG and plan to share with you some stories of some of my closest friends during the years that I was growing up in Madison Heights. I chose to introduce you to Troop 33 first because most of MY GANG were members of that troop, but not all of them. We endured some good times and bad during those years.

BOY SCOUT TROOP 33
Madison Heights Baptist Church, 1951
Left to right: front row: Henry Gouyer, Jr., Benjamin Trevillian, Jimmie Thacker, Allen Whitmore, Ronnie Bryant, Percy Gunter, Walter "Sonny" Apperson, Richard "Wimpy" Pentecost, and Donald Ewers.
Second row: Preston "P.G." Scott, E.W. Woody, Cary Ogden, Edward "Red" Crews, Ralph "Crow" Johnson, Ronnie Rosser, Jimmie Whitten, Jimmie Goff, and Bill Dodgion,
Third row: Lloyd Gunter, Calvin Phelps, Kyle Baldwin, John Lee Smith, Ronald "Buddy" Johnson, Charles Stinson, and John Ragland.
Fourth row: Hugh Wilson (assistant scoutmaster), Donnie Dodgion, Joe Nuckols, Hunter "Mack" Kidd, Raymond Stinson, John "Johnny" Marks, Massie "Petey" Stinson, J.D. Riley, and Jim Hughes (scoutmaster).

TROOP 33 GOING CAMPING
Left to right, Ronnie Bryant, Johnny Marks, Hunter Kidd, Ralph Johnson, Raymond Stinson, Richard Pentecost behind Massie Stinson, Kyle Baldwin behind Paul Manley and Walter Apperson.

As the years have passed, it has been painful to see some of those friends pass from this life. In the picture of Troop 33, there are 34 people. Ten of them are dead and I cannot account for three more. I occasionally see some of the others and when I do, we like to reminisce about our times together in Madison Heights. Let me introduce you to my friends in Boy Scout Troop 33.

Our Monday night scout meetings were great times for us. In addition to the "serious stuff" we enjoyed playing blackout, capture the flag and steal the bacon. We loved it. We would go on camping trips to "Ghost Camp," a log cabin on the river near the Southern Railroad bridge. Often in the summer time, a group of us would go there for an entire week. For those who could afford the cost (I think it was $15), we had the opportunity to go to Scout Camp at Camp Monacan for a week. The camp was owned by the Piedmont Boy Scout Council and located at Nellysford in Nelson County. The Council office was located in the People's Bank Building on the corner of Eighth and Main in Lynchburg and was overseen by Chief Cody. This wonderful camp was sold for the development of Wintergreen, a profitable, but unfortunate decision for the Boy Scouts in our district. The Piedmont Council no longer exists and the Madison Heights area is now served by the Blue Ridge Mountain Council. Troop 33, once a strong troop, now is defunct.

I don't know what kind of event the troop is off to in the picture below. It appears they are going on another camping trip since they have recruited Jack Marks and

ON THE ROAD AGAIN
Left to right, scouts: Raymond Adams, Kyle Baldwin, Percy Gunter, P.G. Scott, Bill Dodgion, David Ramey, unknown, Raymond Stinson, Donald Ewers, Ralph Johnson, Harry Taliaferro, John Ragland, Danny Morcom, Richard Pentecost. Adults: Frank Lang, James Hughes, Charles Irvin and Jack Marks. The old truck belonged to Jack Marks.

CAMP MONACAN AT NELLYSFORD, VA.
Some troop members after high winds destroyed their tent during the middle of the night. (Benjamin Trevillian, unknown, Jimmie Thacker, and Ralph "Crow" Johnson)

his old Dodge truck to carry the baggage. Strangely, his son Johnny Marks isn't in the picture and neither am I so we must have been involved in something else. It isn't strange that Jack got recruited to help even though Johnny isn't present because everybody in the community called on Jack for everything. He was an electrician at Lynchburg Foundry, but got home around three each afternoon and usually had some project to work on each day. Recently, in a conversation with Terry Ray, he mentioned how good Jack was to his family after his dad died. He said they had an antiquated furnace, stoker, and thermostat in their home that Jack kept operational for them for many years for no charge. It wasn't unusual for someone to call him in the middle of the night to come fix a well pump or a furnace. Terry said, "He could fix most anything and I know that many times he never got paid." Even though Jack was a faithful member of Madison Heights Methodist Church, he frequently is seen in pictures of special events at other churches, especially the Baptist church where his wife, Mary, was the church pianist and a Sunday School teacher. Jack was my uncle and lived close to me. He had a great workshop in his basement where I spent many hours when I was growing up.

It wasn't just fun, games, and camping trips for Boy Scout Troop 33. Frequently we were called upon to participate in community and church activities. In the following picture we have joined forces with representatives from the local American Legion unit and volunteers representing every branch of the military for a Memorial Day service at Madison Heights Baptist, our sponsoring church. We also participated in parades and special events in Lynchburg, including some at the Lynchburg City Stadium. We had a great time and owe a lot to the outstanding adult leadership we had.

MEMORIAL DAY SERVICE
Madison Heights Baptist Church, May 27, 1951

Left to right, Recessional: James Hughes (scoutmaster), Hugh Wilson (assistant scoutmaster), Allen Whitmore, Bill Dodgion, Benjamin Trevillian, Richard Pentecost, Ronnie Rosser, Edward Crews, Jimmy Goff, and P.G. Scott.
First row: Donnie Dodgion, Massie Stinson, Calvin Phelps, Ralph "Crow" Johnson, John Ragland, John Lee Smith, Kyle Baldwin, Joe Nuckols, Charles Stinson, and John Marks.
Adults on stage: Marion Irvin, D. Vest, Elmo Baldwin, unknown, unknown Marine Sgt., Robert Ragland, Lucille H. Hughes, and Harry Bryant.

Chapter 25

Our Band

If you visited a home in the South on Saturday night during the second quarter of the twentieth century you would probably find a radio tuned to "The Grand Ole Opry." There were two reasons for this: Country music was King in the south and there were no televisions. My home was no exception. My daddy "couldn't carry a tune in a bucket" as folks used to say, but he loved to listen to country music. Mama had taken piano lessons as a girl and could play a few hymns, but was not an accomplished musician. Some of our family could sing well and some could not. Enough said. I determined that I was going to learn to play the guitar.

Charles with his first guitar

A guitar-playing neighbor taught me some basic chords and allowed me to practice on his guitar. After my brother Robert joined the Navy, he lent me $39 to buy my first Harmony guitar at L. Oppleman. I paid him back a few dollars a week from my part-time job. He had shipped overseas to the Mediterranean for a six-month cruise and wouldn't need his money until he returned home. A good deal for me: family financing with no collateral or interest!

Several of my closest friends shared the same love for music that I did and also the desire to

ROBERT'S SHIP, HEAVY CRUISER U.S.S. MACON
Robert was a gunner in one of the large gun turrets. He served in the Atlantic fleet during the Korean War.

learn to play. Some of them learned to play on my guitar and later bought their own. Whenever they were around, somebody was always playing my guitar. We literally wore out the fret board on it. My home was always the unofficial gathering place for my friends and had been for the friends of my older brothers and sisters. I'm not sure whether it was my parent's long-suffering nature or my mama's cooking! I think it was both. Although many wannabe musicians passed through our doors, our band was eventually composed of Ralph "Crow" Johnson, Lloyd Gunter, my cousin Raymond Stinson and me.

Our band would take advantage of every opportunity we had to see and hear other musicians. Square dances were held locally at the Odd Fellows Hall on Fourth Street several times a year. Ransell Williams, his son Jimmy, and a variety of other players would furnish the music. We would sneak in and sit on the stage with them and watch them play. They didn't mind us being there because we would hold their cigarettes and give them a puff during the long numbers.

When a stage show came to Lynchburg, we did everything possible to attend. They would usually appear at the Isis or the Academy theatres. We were able to see Grandpa Jones, Bill Monroe, Mother Maybelle and the Carter Sisters, Carl Smith, and many lesser-known musicians. Once we went to Roanoke to see an all-star cast: Hank Snow, Faron Young, The Davis Sisters, Hawkshaw Hawkins, and others. They had a young singer with them that we had never heard of. He played a guitar and was accompanied by two men playing an electric guitar and bass. They were awesome. His name was Elvis Presley.

The next time I was in his presence was in Germany when we were both members

OUR BAND
Left to right: Raymond Stinson, Charles Stinson, Lloyd Gunter, and Ralph Johnson. (Daddy is sleeping in the chair, but would never admit he was asleep. Maybe he isn't… he's still holding his pipe!)

Charles Stinson, 1959

of the Third Armored Division (Spearhead). He was a jeep driver in the Seventh Artillery Battalion in Friedburg and I was in a sister battalion, the Third Artillery, in Butzbach. Although I visited Friedburg frequently and we both participated in Division Artillery maneuvers I never saw him again except in the newspaper.

After our band members finished high school, we all went different directions and seldom got together to play. Military, jobs, and marriage separated us. Now two of our band members are dead. A few old pictures and a lot of memories are all that remain besides two nagging questions: Were we as good as we thought we were, and could we have found success as a band? I think we could have, but I'm glad we didn't try. The price for that kind of success is too high.

Chapter 26

Cousins

Growing up with cousins is not an uncommon experience, but growing up with three male cousins of identical ages must be. An additional factor was the closeness of our homes to each other. All four of us lived in separate houses, but I could stand in any one of their yards and easily throw a rock into mine.

Raymond Stinson lived almost directly across Second Street from me. Massie Stinson, Jr. lived on Clark Street beside my other cousin, John Marks, Jr. Unlike my two Stinson cousins, John was the only son of my mother's brother, Jack Marks.

We all began school together, graduated together, played ball, fished, hunted, camped, belonged to the same scout troop and church, and sometimes vacationed together. Although there were other cousins and friends on the scene with us, there was a special bond between us four.

Left to right, front: Johnny Marks and Raymond Stinson. Back: Charles Stinson and Massie Stinson, Jr.

Chapter 27

The Rest of the Gang

One of the first things I realized when I typed the title for this chapter is that it is impossible to include all the friends who touched my life when I was growing up. Sometimes I would "hang out" with my older brothers and sisters and their friends. I do not have pictures of all of them, but I will include some that I have.

We played ball on the hillside above my house. A hit past first base would land in Clark Street. A long drive to center field would hit in Second Street. A weakly hit ball past third base would roll down the hill…and roll…and roll! We played there because daddy allowed it and we had nowhere else to play. We had a wonderful time!

OUR BASEBALL TEAM
Left to right, front row: Leo Bryant, Bill Dodgion. Second row: Donnie Dodgion, and Russell Bryant, Jr. Third row: Massie "Petey" Stinson and Ralph "Crow" Johnson. Back row: Charles Stinson, "Johnny" Marks and his dog Blue. Other two dogs are unidentified.

ROBERT AND FRIENDS
Left to right, front row: Douglas Allen, Robert Stinson, Beverly Eggleston, Edwin "Buzzy" McBride, and Leonard France. Back row: Barbara Ray, Margie Freeman, Lois Arthur, Juanita Duff, Jane Arnold, Carrie Bell Owen, Hattie Kidd, Patricia Perdue and Addie Cyrus.

MARGARET AND FRIENDS
Left to right, front row: Shirley Richardson, Doris Perdue, Shirley Campbell, Tillie Terry, Ann Richardson, and Kitty Scott. Second row: Angeline Adams, Gracie Scott, Margaret Stinson, Minabelle Williams, Mary Jane Lang, and Linwood Lee. Third row: Lucy Ann Wood, Chiquita Wright, Emma Walton, Virginia Lee Irvin, Helen Fulcher, Mary Williams, Virginia Carey and Mabel Cleveland. Fourth Row: Connie Martin, Beverly Eggleston, Robert Stinson, Neil Baldwin, Richard Morcom and Roy Eggleston.

The undated photo on the previous page is a group of Robert's school class members (the Class of 1951) that was probably taken in 1946 or 1947. The location appears to be outside of the seventh-grade classroom of Madison Heights High School and they seem to be about the right age for seventh-graders.

Some of the remaining members of this class meet on the third Wednesday of each month at an area restaurant for a Dutch treat lunch and fellowship. It is usually attended by 12 to 20 people. After the meal, the group decides where they will meet the following month. The group has graciously invited my wife and me to attend and we have found it to be an enjoyable time. I have since learned that other classes who graduated from Madison Heights High School are doing the same thing. I would encourage more groups to consider doing this.

Also pictured on the previous page is the Intermediate Sunday School Department at Madison Heights Baptist Church, 1947. Margaret and Robert were both in this Department at the same time since the age span was about 13 to 17 years of age. Today, they would be classified as Junior and Senior High classes. Mabel Cleveland was the wife of Rev. Curtis P. Cleveland, our pastor, and one of the teachers. Mrs. Emma Walton, Mrs. Linwood Johnson Lee, and Doris Perdue were also teachers.

EARL AND FRIENDS
Left to right, front row: Clarence "Bozy" Harrell and his dog Fritzie, Blake Earl Harrell, and Earl Stinson. (nice shoes brother!)
Back row: Carl Wood, Lawrence Blanks, Jr., and Aubrey Wood.

Earl's friends were about ten years older than me, but they were some of the group who were friends with my brothers. They spent many hours at our home where this picture was taken. Mama said that Blake Harrell came straight to her house every day after school to see what she had been cooking, hoping for some cookies or a cake. She would look up and see him peeking through the glass in the kitchen door!

These boys were the right age for World War II. I know five of them served in the military. When Carl Wood returned home from Europe after the war he came to visit Mom and Dad. He said he used to tell himself when he was overseas, "I'm in no more danger here than I was when I was playing down at Mrs. Stinson's with those guys!"

RALPH AND FRIENDS
Left to right, standing: Glenn Ricketts, George Coleman, Ralph Stinson, Jimmie Davis and Harold Coleman. Seated: Aubrey Wood.

W. Glenn Ricketts Youth Sports Complex

You will probably recognize this as my cover picture. Although Ralph and Earl were close in age and shared a lot of mutual friends, only one person in this picture appears in the picture on the previous page with Earl and that is Aubrey Wood. The car appears to be a 1933 Plymouth sedan. It belonged to Hazel Coleman, George and Harold's sister. It was parked near their home on Main Street.

Some of these men were also in the World War II age bracket or close to it. Ralph received a deferment to finish school in 1946 and then served in the Occupational Forces in Japan immediately after the war. Glenn Ricketts served later in the Navy and was permanently injured in an accident on an aircraft carrier in 1953. After a lengthy rehabilitation he returned home. Confined to a wheelchair, he was unable to play baseball, a sport he loved and played in school and the Navy. His love for the game found an new outlet through Madison Heights Little League baseball, which later became part of Dixie Youth Baseball, Inc. According to Peggy Ricketts, Glenn's wife, he had two dreams. First, he wanted to see the development of a sports complex in Madison Heights for the children. This

Frank, "Tiny," and Friends

was fulfilled with the construction of The W. Glenn Ricketts Youth Sports Complex which was named in his honor. His second dream was to host a Dixie Youth Baseball World Series at this site. This dream was fulfilled in August 2001, but because of failing health, Glenn only attended one game. He died on September 20, 2001. Madison Heights was honored the second time when it was chosen again six years later to host the 2007 Dixie Youth Baseball World Series.

The Boat Landing on the James River (chapter four) was a favorite place for fishing, boating, picnics, and swimming for young and old alike. This picture was taken there on July 2, 1939. Left to right are Walker Freeman, Jr., Bernice Mayberry, Virginia Mayberry, Dorothy "Tiny" Stinson (kneeling), Frank Stinson (standing behind "Tiny") and "Johnny Man" Mayberry. Although they look older, they were Juniors and Seniors in high school when this picture was taken. I have included a sampling of all of my siblings and some of their friends in this book. I wish it were possible to include more, but space and availability of pictures make it unfeasible. I am grateful for the old photos of their friends and for those who were willing to share them. Because of their association with my brothers and sisters I can also call them my friends.

A NEIGHBORHOOD BIRTHDAY PARTY 1942
Left to right, front row: Buckie Tyree, Emily Harris, Ann Mays, Geraldine Stinson, Charles Stinson, Warren Moon. Second row: Corrine Tyree, unknown, unknown, Petey Stinson, and Raymond Stinson. Third row: Bobby Woody, Peggy Woody unknown, and Alice Farish.

Chapter 28

Recreation

Hunting, fishing, and swimming were some of the favorite pastimes in our family. Some of us played baseball and we loved to attend baseball games, but the above three sports were the ones we participated in the most.

I killed my first deer at age 15. Earl belonged to a hunt club in Rockbridge County and I went hunting with him as his guest. I missed a week from school to go. Since deer were not so plentiful in 1951 as they are now, I returned home a hero. Most everyone at school was impressed except one teacher, Mrs. Edythe Fraley. She threatened to fail me for the year, but didn't.

The James River always provided plenty of activity for my brothers, our friends and me. We fished it day and night, usually walking anywhere we wanted to go. Footpaths led over every ridge and through each hollow. Even though the river was very polluted, we believed the false teaching that "running water purified itself after so many feet." We would stay away from the places where we knew sewage entered the river and go elsewhere to fish, boat, or swim. Earl and Curtis Mayberry also ran a trap line for several years catching

Charles Stinson, 1951

Walter Carroll

Sam Holt

muskrats for pelts. I went with him a few times when I was small. When I asked him recently whose boat he used, he said "Any of them that was unlocked, but mostly Sam Tyree's."

Sometimes he would use one of the boats to take Walter Carroll fishing. Walter would fish and Earl would pole the boat. To return the favor, Walter took Earl to town to sell his muskrat hides. A buyer routinely came to the Sears and Roebuck store on Main Street to buy pelts. The first time the buyer paid Earl, he gave him a check. Earl was disappointed and told Walter, "I thought that man was going to pay me with money." Walter laughed and said, "Come on, I'll get you some money for it." They went to Lynchburg National Bank on the corner of Ninth and Main where our neighbor, Sam Holt, worked. Earl got his money, but not before Walter told Sam and everyone else who cared to listen what Earl had said about the check. Earl was embarrassed.

I always loved to fish and I thought I would spend more time fishing when I retired instead of writing books. I caught a two and a half pound catfish in the river near "The Flat Rock" when I was 12 years old. This is in the area currently being considered for the development of a Riverfront Park by Amherst County. This was a large fish for that time, but is no comparison to the large flathead cats that are now caught there. Fishing in the James River is better today than it has been in my lifetime thanks to the good management of the Virginia Department of Game and Inland Fishing and cleaner water. May it continue to improve.

Several years ago I took a walk down the river looking for some of the old landmarks that I knew when I was a boy. Many of them were destroyed or changed by the expansion of the Smiley Block Company and the installation of a sewer line from Madison Heights to Lynchburg. I was pleased to find The Flat Rock had not been covered by debris. It was a wonderful place to fish from, but only accessible when the water was low. Located several feet from the shore, we could step on other rocks to reach the 10-foot diameter rock and would sit there while we fished downstream. The water level in the river fluctuated as the power plant at Reusens opened or closed its gates. We had to keep an eye on the water level to be sure we didn't get trapped on the rock by the rising water.

Charles Stinson, 1947

Swimming was also an important part of our lives. We swam in the river, the creeks, the city pools and the lakes. Family outings at Holiday Lake and Bedford Lake were common for us. Our school sponsored a Junior/Senior picnic each year at Holiday Lake. Madison Heights Baptist Church also sponsored an occasional picnic there. In between these events, the river provided a place to fish, boat and swim.

This 1939 picture shows two of my brothers at the river. Earl is in the water and Frank is in the boat. Notice N & W stenciled on the boat. The boats were privately owned by the men who worked for the railroad on Percival's Island, but they stenciled their boats thinking the logo may deter a thief from taking them.

Frank and Earl Stinson

Beck Creek below Brightwell's Mill

Tubing

There were two other streams that we loved to go to for swimming. One was Pedlar River and the other was Beck Creek below Brightwell's Mill. Because there were no deep holes of water in either of them they were perfect for small children and non-swimmers.

These pictures were taken at Beck Creek below Brightwell's Mill in the mid-1940s. From front to rear Geraldine Stinson, my mother Viola, with "Kitty" Scott behind her. My daddy, Herman is shown next with Raymond Stinson on his left. The one in the back is Massie "Petey" Stinson. Neither of my parents could swim, but they would take us to the creeks or lakes and sometimes pack a picnic lunch for everyone.

One of our greatest joys was to persuade someone with a car to take us to one of these locations for a cool dip on a hot day. The water was usually cold, especially Pedlar, but pollution was not a worry. Some folks would get excited when they came face to face with a water snake in the water, but usually the snake made a quick exit from all the noise that was generated. The worst creek for snakes was Williams Run on Wright Shop Road. We would ride our bikes there to swim or seine for minnows. Lots of snakes!

The swimming hole at Beck Creek was ideal for floating on a

tube as you see me doing here. This is the most likely time that you would encounter a water snake swimming on top of the water. A friend of mine had one crawl up on the tube behind him and he was unaware of it until his companions on the bank informed him of the hitchhiker. He put on quite a show for them! Contrary to what most people believe, water snakes we find in our area streams are not venomous, but are foul-tempered. They may make people hurt themselves getting away from them.

Our excursions to the lake would usually involve several families and carloads of people. Although Bedford and Holiday lakes were the ones we frequented the most, occasionally we would go to Douthat State Park or Cave Mountain Lake.

This picture was taken at Cave Mountain Lake on one of our family outings. My brother Robert is on the left and my sister Margaret is sitting behind me. This was not one of our favorite lakes because the water was always so cold. On this particular outing several of my married siblings went along with their families. Regardless of the water temperature, the food and fellowship was always great.

Television is the number one form of entertainment in America today. I'm sure that one of the reasons we found other forms of amusement is because there were no televisions (or at least they weren't widely available) when these pictures were taken. One of the first people in the community to own a television was Charles Irvin who lived on Main Street. He and his wife, Lucille, would graciously allow people to come and watch boxing on Friday nights. If everyone couldn't get in the house, they would stand on the porch and watch through the window. The picture would fade out often or be filled with snow, but it was a real treat to see this new invention.

Cave Mountain Lake, 1947

Little did we know how television would revolutionize our lives and our culture. Pabst Blue Ribbon Beer was one of the sponsors of Friday night boxing and soon every kid in town could sing the commercial song: *"What'll you have? Pabst Blue*

Charles and Lucille Irvin

Margaret and Charles Stinson, 1939-40

Ribbon…Pabst Blue Ribbon Beer." One family moved away from Madison Heights and joined a church in their new community. When the minister was introducing them he asked their young son what he liked to do. The boy said he liked to sing and began to sing the Pabst Blue Ribbon song to the shock of his parents and the delight of the people.

I should also mention how much we enjoyed snow in the winter. We would ride our sleds from daylight to dark if our parents would permit it, but they seldom did. We still had our chores to do and sometimes we would have to quit just to get warm and dry. We never had the luxury of spare gloves or waterproof boots, but we would bundle up in what we had and go as long as we could before coming in to warm up, dry out, and grab a snack.

The sled we are riding belonged to our family, courtesy of my uncle, Wiley Marks. It was one of the best sleds in the community and saw much use. It had some bloodstains on its underside where one of Wiley's friends came down Stumps Hill on it and ran under the rear of the bus. Ouch! He lost a few teeth in that round. One of Earl's friends was sledding in our yard on a fast track after dark and ran up on the front porch. He hit the front door so hard it flew open and he ended up in our living room. "Hello!" These were exceptions; mostly we stayed between the ditches and had lots of fun.

There were more kids than there were sleds in our neighborhood so we had to take turns sledding. This almost caused a serious problem in December 1935. My oldest sister, Dorothy, (we called her "Tiny,") was sledding two blocks from home when Mama sent word for her to come home as quickly as she could. It was almost her turn to ride the sled and she didn't want to lose her turn so she waited to ride before leaving. When she came home, Mama was excited and angry. She needed "Tiny" to take the younger children to Alice Bryant's house "Quick!" Why? I was about to be born.

There are some other interesting things in the previous picture that I don't want readers to overlook. In the background, there are outdoor toilets visible in two of our neighbors' yards. For those who never had one, try to imagine what it would be like on a cold, snowy, day to have to go out there every time you had to use the bathroom. Notice how far they are from the houses, which was a good thing in the summer time and a bad thing in the winter. You figure out why. The little building in the upper right-hand corner with the hip roof is a well house. Inside was a hand dug well where you drew your water with a rope, pulley, and bucket. Were the well and toilet located too close together? Probably, but practicality usually prevailed.

This well house also had two burlap bags (but everybody called them "crocus sacks"), hanging by nails on a sidewall. These were used to store empty food cans in until the bags were filled. They were then carried to "the dump," which was located on a vacant lot on Horseford Road adjacent to our property. Carrying the two bags of cans to "the dump" for our neighbor was a good way for me to earn a quarter. A quarter would provide me transportation to Lynchburg and back on the bus, and a twelve-cent ticket to the Trenton for a movie. If I walked one way I could use that nickel to buy me a drink and still have three cents left to spend on penny candy at Wright's store. For those who doubt that I could go to the Trenton Theatre for 12 cents, take a look at the ticket. Even back then we had to pay 20 percent tax.

Trenton Theatre Ticket

Now for a bit of trivia. While writing this article I began to wonder why people called the bags "crocus sacks" or "croaker sacks". After I couldn't find an answer, I enlisted the help of my two sons, Mike and Tim. Together they found several possible answers, but Mike finally located what we believe is the right one on the following Website.

From thefreedictionary.com/gunnysack "According to Craig M. Carver, who draws on the research of Walter S. Avis, '*Crocus* is a coarse, loosely woven material once worn by slaves and laborers and common in colonial New England. It probably took its name from the sacks in which crocus or saffron was shipped.' Though the term *crocus sack* virtually disappeared from New England by the endof the 19th century, it survives in the South."

Before I move away from recreation, I feel it would be good to mention the additional opportunities that were available when I was old enough to get a car. I look back fondly at the three different automobiles I owned when I was single and wish I still had them. The first was a 1947 Plymouth Club Coupe that I paid $300 dollars for in 1954. My daddy loaned me the money because I needed a car to get to work.

| 1947 Plymouth | 1951 Ford Hardtop | 1956 Ford Fairlane |

MY FIRST THREE CARS

Playing shuffleboard at Bill's Barn

It was a nice, dependable car, but not the flashy machine that I dreamed of (although I saw one for sale recently for $5,000). After I paid it off, I traded it for a 1951 Ford, two-door hardtop. It was sharp looking, but never mechanically right. When I paid it off, I traded if for a brand new 1956 Ford Fairlane. Wow, what a car! It was pretty, dependable, and fast! Everything I wanted. Wish I still had it.

Cars provided my friends and me the opportunity to launch out for new horizons. Dates, vacations at the beach, automobile races at Darlington and Martinsville, hunting and fishing trips, or just hanging out at the drive-in theatres and drive-in restaurants that were so popular in the 1950s, all became options once I had a car. Lynchburg had Hollins Mill, The Southerner, and Jumbo drive-in restaurants. Madison Heights had Bill's Barn, a converted barn operated by Billy Merryman, and a favorite hangout for my crowd. Some evenings, we would just cruise around to all of them. We also had our own drive-in-theatre. Amherst Drive-In-Theatre was located where Monelison Elementary School is now. Life was good.

Occasionally, someone from our community would go on a fishing trip to the ocean. Some of my family members liked to fish from a fishing pier when we were at the beach or fish in the inlets with a small rented boat, but we never went deep-sea fishing. On Labor Day weekend, 1958, three people from Madison Heights and several from Lynchburg went deep-sea fishing near Cape Henry, Virginia. The group caught 33 dolphins and one blue marlin. Jimmie Williams, his brother, Ed Williams, and George Deaton were the lucky anglers from our community. Jimmie was the one who caught the six-foot, nine-inch marlin.

SIX-FOOT, NINE-INCH BLUE MARLIN
Left to right, George Deaton, Ed Williams, and Jimmie Williams

PART FIVE:
Miscellaneous

Chapter 29

The Influence of the Churches

Only eternity will tell how much influence the churches of Madison Heights had upon its people. When our boys went off to war, many of them were grounded in the Christian faith they had learned in one of the four churches in our community. The Baptists, Methodists, Episcopalians, and Disciples of Christ all had active congregations. Today, only two of the original congregations remain in Old Town.

Madison Heights Baptist Church

This is the church I attended when I was growing up in Madison Heights. My daddy taught Sunday School there for 43 years. I was ordained there as a Deacon and later as a Minister of the Gospel. This building served from 1923 until 1967. Even though this building has been replaced, the congregation is still strong and an influence in the community. This church holds many fond memories for me.

ANNIVERSARY CELEBRATION, 1951
Jimmie Ray took this picture and the following two at the 60th anniversary celebration service in 1951. We "old timers" can easily identify many of those pictured, but because almost six decades have passed most of the adults in the pictures are no longer alive. Montague Nicholas and W.W. Freeman are seated on the front row. Jack Marks is operating the lights from the left side of the balcony

This shows the cast of players that was in the pageant presented to the church. Rev. Curtis P. Cleveland and his wife Mabel are the second and third persons on the left in the front row. The three women standing behind them from left to right are Vera Bryant, pianist Mary Marks, and Ruth Cook, organist and choir director. Mr. Pete Kessler is in the center of the first row and Emma Bryant is on his left. Both of them were charter members. Mrs. Russell Woody and Miss Jesse Paris are standing behind them. From right to left in the front row are Kathleen Campbell, Mrs. Sam Adams, and Virginia Campbell. Standing behind Virginia is Dorothy Baldwin. The first three children sitting on the steps are (left to right) Judy Paulette, Gloria Cleveland, and Betty Sue Nicholas.

The Influence of the Churches

Neil Baldwin is at the piano; Anne Rosser is on the end of the third row over Neil's shoulder. The four boys on the front row are Emmett Murphy, Peyton Cleveland, Danny Morcom and Johnny Fulcher. Geraldine Stinson (with scarf in 2nd row) has Kitty Scott and Barbara Stinson on her left.

C.T. Phelps and William "Bill" Cook, Sr.

Among my memories of Madison Heights Baptist Church are the faithful people. I wish I could include all of them in this book, but that is impossible. Because this picture has been made available to me, I have chosen to let these two men serve as representatives of all the others. I believe all those others, would agree with my choice. During the 35 years I attended there, I always expected to see certain people present for the services. The men above are two of those people. I already mentioned the exceptional work ethic of Charlie Phelps in chapter four. The same could be said for Bill Cook. I want to emphasize the commitment these men had to their church, employers, community, and families. That which we may consider outstanding today, they considered normal. I thank God for them and the legacy they left us.

While researching this book, I found many pictures of young people from the Madison Heights community involved in activities that had been organized and carried out with the help of various organizations and volunteer adult leaders. Some were sponsored by churches, schools, or civic organizations, while others were individually sponsored. I have tried to include some of each. There are other excellent group pictures I could have used, but I have tried to avoid duplication so that I could include as many different people as possible. The picture below of a breakfast meeting of the Intermediate Department at Madison Heights Baptist Church is a classic example of a church sponsored event. I do not know the exact date of this late 1940s meeting or the purpose. It is probably more than a fellowship meeting since they had a guest speaker.

INTERMEDIATE DEPARTMENT BREAKFAST
Madison Heights Baptist Church Fellowship Hall
Left to right, seated: Linwood Johnson, Doris Perdue, Patricia Perdue, Faye Gillispie, guest speaker (unknown), Barbara Ray, Lois Arthur, Emma Walton, Bennie Walton, William "Bill" Cook, Sr. Standing: Donald Owen, Roy Eggleston, Neil Baldwin, Lois Goodman, Mary Jane Lang, Richard Goodman, Hallie Godsey, Shirley Cooper, Frank Murphy, Jr., Tillie Terry, Connie Martin and James Morcom.

FORMER PASTORS AT THE BAPTIST CHURCH

REV. CURTIS P. CLEVELAND FAMILY 1944–1954
Gloria, Grover, Mable Cleveland, Rev. Curtis Cleveland and Peyton.

REV. FLOY W. COX FAMILY 1955–1960
Judy, Ruth Cox, Rev. Floy Cox and Debbie

Rev. Hugh Bumgarner and family
Left to right, Donna, Ardie, Alan, and Rev. Hugh Bumgarner, September 7, 1960

Rev. Hugh Bumgarner was called to be pastor of Madison Heights Baptist Church in 1960 and served for 32 years, the longest tenure of any pastor of that church. After retiring, he continued to serve in interim positions and is currently serving as pastor of Midway Baptist Church in Piedmont Baptist Association.

Although I was baptized by Mr. Cleveland and married by Mr. Cox, it was Mr. Bumgarner that made the greatest impact on my life. He recognized the leadership abilities that God had given me and encouraged me to develop them. When I was interested in working with the Boy Scouts, he guided me into the Royal Ambassador program. Under his guidance I became a Sunday School teacher, was ordained a deacon, licensed to preach, and ordained a Minister of the Gospel. I thank him for the patient leadership he gave to me.

Madison Heights Methodist Church

This beautiful building still stands on the corner of Fifth and Church Streets, but another congregation, the Solid Rock Baptist Church, currently uses it for worship. It was built in 1872 and rebuilt in 1903. The Methodist congregation chose to move from their Old Town location. They merged with the congregation of Bailey's Chapel Methodist Church and the two groups built a new building on Amelon Road and called it Amelon United Methodist Church. The first service was held in the new church building on October 13, 1996.

There was a small softball field behind the original church that served well for the church teams and also for the local kids to play on. The large basement room and kitchen provided a meeting place for church social activities, wedding receptions, and community organizations. A Boy Scout troop met there briefly and found it to be an excellent area for indoor games. The Odd Fellows and Rebeccas Banquet pictured in Chapter 14 took place there and many other organizations used it at various times.

YOUNG WOMEN'S CHORUS, 1945
Left to right, front row: Rev. Ernest E. Emurian, Louise Doss, Sammie Holley, Hazel Bryant, Mary Jane Holt, Nina Wood, Hulda Woody, Mildred Ricketts, Margaret Holt, Martha Wood, Frankie Farmer (director)
Second row: Joyce Kirkpatrick, Joyce Wright, Carla Crews, Betsy Hudnall, Dorothy McLane, Arlene Kirkpatrick, Virginia Hudnall.
Third row: Francis Shrader, Vivian Shrader, Mary Eva McBride, Kathryn Bryant, Nancy Woody, and Ann Coleman.
(Names supplied by Sammie Holley Stinson)

Rev. F. O. Briggs

Rev. F.O. Briggs was the beloved pastor of Madison Heights Methodist Church from 1947 until 1970, an exceptionally long tenure for a Methodist minister. In addition to providing pastoral care to his flock, he was very involved in civic and community activities.

Rev. Briggs loved to visit the nearby post office in the afternoon and interact with the people waiting for their mail. While talking with him one afternoon about a funeral he had recently conducted he said to me, "Charles, the time is coming when funerals will be held at night and the family and funeral director will go to the cemetery the next day to bury the body. I won't live long enough to see it, but you probably will." I remembered his words almost 50 years later when I conducted my first night funeral. I was discussing this with a funeral director several years ago and he was telling me that the latest trend in other states is "drive-by visitation." The body is displayed behind a glass window. Visitors drive-by for the viewing, sign the register, and drive away. I wonder what Mr. Briggs would think of that?

MADISON HEIGHTS CHRISTIAN CHURCH
This church is located at 149 Main Street and still conducts weekly services. Rev. G. C. Looney, pictured at right, was one of its early pastors, serving many years.

MADISON HEIGHTS EPISCOPAL CHURCH
This small picturesque church building still stands on Main Street between Fifth and Sixth. The last Episcopal congregation to use the building had dwindled to only a few families before they disbanded. The death of older members combined with the relocation of most of the younger ones led to its demise.
Several congregations of different faiths have used the building since the Episcopal Church closed. Most of them relocated or closed after a brief period of operation. Currently it is being used by a congregation called the Jesus Center Apostolic Holiness Church.

EASTER SUNDAY
The date of this Easter Sunday service in the Madison Heights Episcopal Church is unknown. The fourteen worshipers in this picture are:
Front: "Sonny" Banton (others are listed left to right)
Second row: Barbara Wright, Linwood Wright
Third row: Viola Banton, Catherine Spivey
Fourth row: Florence Banton, Hallie Wright, Callie Wright, Christine Banton
Fifth row: Tom Banton, Walter Wright, Hume Cox (Pastor), Ray Spivey, Floyd Stevens

Chapter 30

Shrader Field

Shrader Field, was owned by Judge Lucien Shrader and was located where Seminole Shopping Center is today. It was the site of a baseball field and a half-mile dirt racetrack for automobiles and horses. The dirt track was replaced with a one-quarter-mile asphalt track that quickly became obsolete when the Amateur and Sportsman racecars were displaced by the stock cars which evolved into the NASCAR we know today. It was also a fairground where county fairs, carnivals, circuses, and "hell drivers" who would perform death defying feats like jumping ramp-to-ramp in automobiles.

A carnival beside the racetrack, 1949

Shrader Field office

MADISON HEIGHTS "RED BIRDS"
Class A League Champions 1944, Duval Shaner, Manager
Left to right, front row: Linwood "Slug" Morris, Lawrence Blanks, Jr., Lewis Loving, Duval Shaner, Page Farmer (bat boy), Norman Dawson (Captain), Claude Duff, Jimmy Williams, Harry "Jr." Singleton. Back row: Sam Owens third base coach, Jack Wingfield, "Rick" Hawkins, Dave Cyrus, Paul Roberts, Leonard Spivey, Houston Argenbright, Carl Farmer, and Wilbur Goff, (first base coach).

Shrader Field was also the home field for the Madison Heights Red Birds baseball team. Thanks to Sterling W. Fitzgerald for supplying the names of the team members.

The Skating Rink was one of the most popular spots at Shrader Field and continued in operation until it was destroyed by fire in the early 1960's.

No story about Madison Heights in the mid-twentieth century would be complete

The skating rink

Pure Oil Station

without mentioning the Pure Oil Station at Shrader Field. It was built in the early 1950s and operated by Bill Brown. It quickly became the gathering place for people my age and older. It was simply known to us as "The Station." One elderly lady who lived nearby called it "the lodestone" because of the way it attracted us.

When the service station was first built, the race track, the skating rink, a restaurant, and several other businesses were also located there. Duval Shaner ran a business there that sold and serviced radios and televisions. His wife, Sadie, ran a restaurant next door. The above picture of the Pure Oil Station was taken in the 1960s. All the original buildings had been replaced except the service station, which was operated by Loy Banton. It soon met its demise also. A book could be written about the things

Sadie Shaner and her coffee shop

that took place at "The Station."

"Sadie's Coffee Shop" advertised fried chicken, steaks, chops, sandwiches, and frozen custard in the above pictures. Later, Charlie Howard and his wife operated the restaurant for many years. They had booths and a counter with stools. The State troopers frequently ate there. It was a good way for them to keep an eye on us young drivers and know who's who and what we were driving. It was also a good way for us to know where they were. If we wanted to take a fast spin up the road, the ideal time to go was while Troopers Daniels, Bayliss, Tipton, or Turpin were eating.

Jean and Lillian were the daughters of Duval and Sadie Shaner, mentioned earlier in this chapter. This picture was taken on the opening night of a new skating rink built and operated by their parents. Their younger brother, Clarence, is shown in chapter 14 as the batboy with the Deluxe Cleaner's championship softball team. Lillian and Jean were also members of that team. These two young ladies were involved in many school and community activities and their pictures appear several times in this book.

Shaner's Radio and Television store and Newcomb's Grocery

Chapter 31

The Old Homeplace

My research for this book required that I search through old family photo albums. I have been surprised by some of the pictures I've found of people and places I had forgotten. I'm sure some of them would be of interest to others, but there are limitations on how many of them I can share.

In addition to raising pigs and a large garden, our family also raised chickens and owned a milk cow. When most of the kids were gone from home, Daddy decided to sell the cow. I was glad! Ralph and Robert were the expert milkers in the family, but I never did conquer that skill.

Even though I was the youngest, I helped with the cow. My first job was carrying buckets of water from the well to fill her drinking tub, located 100 feet away in the cow lot. We also kept the one above beside the well. When we had the cow out grazing her, we would usually water her before putting her back in the lot. It saved carrying a lot of water by hand. When I carried water, I would usually end up with wet pants legs and water in my shoes. This was only a problem in the winter because I went barefoot in the summer, but

Ralph and Gypsy

what worse time to have wet legs and feet? I believe that old cow was kin to a camel; she could hold a lot of water! I also would take her out to graze when the grass in the small pasture was scarce, but I never had to milk like the others.

Grazing a cow may sound like a nice relaxing job for those who are inclined to be dreamers or have some romantic notions of communing with nature while listening to the steady munch of a hungry cow devouring grass. Before you rush out and buy a cow let me tell you the down side to such a venture. Consider the logistics. A 75-pound boy on one end of a chain or rope is no match for a 1000-pound cow on the other. The cow wore a halter with the rope or chain hooked to a ring on it. It doesn't have the same stopping power as a bit in a horse's mouth. When the cow decides she's going to get a few bites out of Daddy's vegetable garden or Mama's prize flowers, guess what happens? Which is better, a rope or chain? Depends on whether you want burns or bruises. The cow doesn't care.

I've already mentioned our many vegetable gardens. Unfortunately, there was one just outside the pasture gate. When we were taking the cow out to graze, she would plod along peacefully until she got beside the garden and then she would lunge into it and grab whatever she could while we tried to pull her out. Daddy decided to put a stop to it so one evening he installed a fence with one strand of barbed wire on it. He thought that would deter her and it did. There was one problem. I was at my neighbors playing when he installed the fence so I didn't know about it. My playmate and I decided to go to our garden and get a carrot to eat, which we frequently did. It was twilight and we were running. I was leading the way and ran into the fence. It was the perfect height to catch me in the mouth. I still have the scar in the corner of my mouth; everyone was glad it wasn't my eye.

Let me tell you one more disadvantage I remember about owning a cow before you rush out and buy one. They have to be bred and have a calf so they will continue to produce an abundance of milk. If you don't breed them, they will routinely (I don't know the frequency) be "bully" and demand to be bred by bellowing for days. You and everyone in the community will know about it. If they aren't bred, they will eventually dry up and give no milk. So the routine is: breed the crazy cow before she drives everybody mad, let her have a calf, wean the calf and sell it, have milk for the family, and repeat the process when needed.

I suppose the process may be simpler today with artificial insemination, but our only choice was to take the cow to a bull. The closest bull was on the Wright Shop Road farm of Mr. Bibb Ewers. How do you get a crazy, bullying cow to Mr. Ewer's farm? One of the boys (usually the oldest available one) hooked the old cow to the end of the rope or chain and walked three miles to the farm, paid the $1 fee, let the bull breed the cow, and walked the cow home. How long did it take? All day. Did I ever have to do it? No. I was too young, but I always dreaded the day when my turn would come. Daddy sold the cow first and I was delighted. If you want to hear a first hand account, talk to my brother Ralph.

One of my other jobs was delivering milk. There were times when we had excess milk and neighbors were always anxious to buy it. We sold it for twelve cents a quart. Mama had acquired surplus glass dairy bottles and had proper caps for them. She prepared the bottles and I delivered them. One of my customers was the Elmer Mayberry family. They had an old dog named Flip and we hated each other. He didn't like me coming in his yard and I didn't like him being alive. When he saw me coming, he started growling and barking. I would stop at the edge of the yard and wait until somebody came outside to provide safety for me to come further. He bit me once so I developed a mental list of bad things I'd like to see happen to old Flip, but none of them ever happened. Much to my sorrow Flip was still there growling and barking at me when we sold the cow and went out of the milk business.

THE ELMER MAYBERRY FAMILY
Left to right, front row: Alfred, Paul, Russell (Dick), Jesse (J.B.), and Mr. Elmer Mayberry. Back row: Curtis, Virginia, Essie, Mamie, Bernice, Myrtle Francis, and Mrs. Myrtle Turner Mayberry. (This picture was taken on October 12, 1946 on the occasion of the marriage of J.B. Mayberry to Pauline Harris)

Robert and Charles with Polly

The chickens

This picture shows Robert (left) and me (right) with Polly, the last cow we owned. She was a good-natured cow, but like all cows she would sometimes step on your foot and then just stand there. Or, she would kick at a fly and stick her foot in the bucket of milk. Or, swat you in the head with her tail full of cockle burrs while you were trying to milk her. I would often try to run interference while Robert milked, but the cow usually won. Now you know why I was glad when Daddy decided to sell her.

After we sold the cow I had a hard time adjusting to the taste of pasteurized dairy milk since I had drunk raw milk all of my life. I had gotten by at school by drinking orange juice instead of milk. Once the cow was gone, I had to drink the store-bought stuff. I eventually acquired a taste for it and several years later when I tasted raw milk again I though it tasted awful. We also had to adjust to not having homemade butter and buttermilk. The latter was no problem for me since I've never liked buttermilk.

I barely remember the chickens, but we had a small flock that provided eggs and occasionally, fried chicken. For the uninformed, the transition from live chicken to fried chicken is worth studying! We had a nice chicken house with a fenced lot, but the chickens would still get out and scratch in the garden or Mama's flower gardens. Mama loved her flowers and worked hard to raise them. The chickens worked equally as hard to escape and get every new seed that she planted. Once, after a hard day of preparing a flowerbed and planting her precious seeds, the chickens got out and destroyed it. That did it! When daddy came home from work, mama had her declaration ready. Those chickens had to go. I don't recall all the conversation, but I know Daddy wanted to keep the chickens and Mama didn't. The next day was Saturday and Daddy only worked half-days. He came home with a chicken crate and told us kids to catch all the chickens and put them in the crate. He drove away with them tied to the luggage rack on the back of the car and returned several hours later with no chickens or crate. When we asked what happened to them, he said, "I threw them in the river." We knew that

Madison Heights post office, 1943, B.H. Bryant's Store is on the right.

Virginia Campbell, postmaster

wasn't true, but nobody ever knew what he did with the chickens. We guessed he took them to The Community Market in Lynchburg and sold them.

One job we all shared when growing up was going to the Post Office four blocks away. It wasn't uncommon to hear your name called followed by the command "go get the mail." The mail would arrive late in the afternoon. The Post Office window would be closed until the mail was "put up." As you might guess, none of these times were specific but usually occurred around four o'clock. When the mail was "put up" the window would reopen and those waiting in the lobby would be served on a "first come" basis.

Mail delivery still continues to be an important part of people's lives although it is performed differently today. In the days when the Madison Heights Post Office was located in Old Town, it was a gathering spot for the locals. It was a place to meet friends and hear the latest news while you waited for your mail. It was also a favorite place for the town ministers to visit and interact with community folks. It was a great time for them to catch up with delinquent members!

For families with members in the military, letters were the primary source of communications. I spent 20 months in Germany and never made a phone call or visit home. During the war years, a phone call or telegram usually came from the Red Cross and meant bad news. We looked forward to those letters from our family members.

During World War II, my two older brothers served overseas. Frank served in the Philippines in the Army and Earl served in Newfoundland in the Navy. The letter below is a 1944 letter from Frank to Ralph. Servicemen were able to mail their letters during the war with no postage. The letter below has "Free" written in the right corner instead of a stamp.

Ralph served in the occupational forces in Japan after World War Two, Robert served during the Korean War and I served in Germany during the Cold War, 1959-61. My uncle, Wiley Marks, was also in the Navy and barely missed the bombing of Pearl Harbor because his ship was at sea. He made a career of the navy, serving during World War Two and the Korean War. He retired as a Lieutenant Commander. He is pictured on the next page with his wife Wertie.

Probably the dominant emotion felt by a young man or woman when they are faced with the reality of leaving home is ambivalence. The difficult task of preparing a child to enter an adult world is a process that begins at birth. Some folks do a much better job than others.

Frank Stinson

Earl Stinson

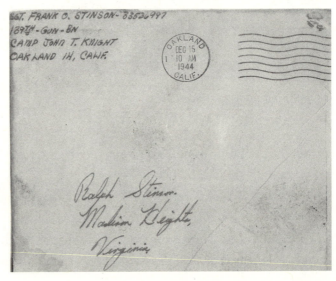

Ralph Stinson

Robert Stinson

Charles Stinson

Wiley Marks

I still remember how it feels to report for work the first day on a new job. I also remember how it felt to be sworn into the Army and then board a bus wondering what tomorrow would bring. I remember boarding a plane for Germany knowing that I probably wouldn't return for almost two years. I approached each of these life events and others with the assurance that I was well prepared for what I would face.

I am thankful that my parents gave me the freedom to participate in so many activities while I was growing up. Each of the activities were learning experiences for me and helped prepare me for the day I would leave home and assume my role in an adult world. They also helped equip me for the day that I would become a parent and could pass on to my children the lessons learned from my experiences.

PART SIX:
What Does the Future Hold?

Chapter 32

Gloom, Doom, or Transformation?

A popular song several decades ago told the story of someone returning to his old hometown and finding it looked the same. I believe that only happens in a fantasy world. It has not happened in my hometown. When I return to Madison Heights and see the neighborhood I grew up in, it is not the same. Many of the old houses are gone. Some have been replaced by mobile homes while other lots are empty except for clutter. Few of the older houses that remain are in good repair and some are boarded up. A few descendants of the old families still live there, tenaciously hanging on to their property, concerned about what the future may bring.

But all is not gloom and doom! In the past few years there has been a renewed interest in Old Town Madison Heights. This has taken place on several fronts. First, people are taking notice of this historical area and wanting to do something to help it. The series of articles that appeared in the *New Era Progress* that I referred to in Chapter 2 has helped serve

Main Street Madison Heights

KYLE BALDWIN

FOUR TEENAGERS
Nancy Campbell, Bonnie Banton, Julia Manley and Kay Crews

Frank Taliaferro and Binky Banton

as a catalyst to increase interest in the area. Some of the suggestions for improvement offered by Editor David Hylton have taken root. Secondly, current residents are appealing to county officials for help for their neighborhood and receiving promises for action.

In addition, new families have purchased some of the older homes, moved into them, and are renovating them. Amherst County is putting into action a new inspection policy for rental houses. Those residents who already take pride in their property are continuing to set an example for those who are not and are letting their voices be heard about the neglect around them. Some middle-aged people who grew up there but moved away are returning to make it their home again.

During the 2007 Christmas season, it was exciting to read about the plans of Madison Heights Baptist Church to conduct a Christmas caroling event in Old Town. This report was followed in the January 20, 2008 newsletter with acknowledgements from two other groups in response to the community ministry of this church. A note from the "Old Town Community Action Group" thanked the congregation for the use of their church facility for their monthly meetings and gave a glowing report about progress being made in the community. A second note from Amherst County Department of Social Services thanked them for their "generous care during the Christmas season for those less fortunate in Amherst County" and went on to add "your participation in Operation Happy Face made the holidays brighter for many children in our community."

The church also provides space in their building for a satellite office for the Amherst County Sheriff's Department. Currently, plans are being made for the congregation

THE GOOD OLD DAYS
Betty Terry, Peyton Cleveland, Eugene Taliaferro, and Carolyn Banton

to sponsor a block party for the neighborhood close to the church. In May 2008, Habitat for Humanity will begin construction on two new homes on vacant lots on Main Street. The church is recruiting workers to assist in this project.

Hopefully, other churches and organizations will use creative ideas like these to provide opportunities to bond with the people of the community that produce positive results in their lives as well as an improved neighborhood. Dr. Timothy Madison, pastor of Madison Heights Baptist Church, and the people of the church are to be commended for their ministry.

As mentioned in an earlier chapter, a combined effort by Amherst County leaders, concerned alumni of Madison Heights High School, and private enterprise, is aimed at restoring the old school buildings on Phelps Road to their former glory. It is their goal that once again these buildings may be a place that will contribute to the well-being of the community and not its decay.

In addition, area and state leaders are working together to obtain funds to assist Old Town residents in their efforts to transform their community. I am not so naïve that I believe Madison Heights will ever return to the way it was during my childhood there, nor should it. But, I do believe it can become a community of people who take pride in who they are and the place that they call home.

Most of the sidewalk that runs the length of Main Street is still intact. Our doctors tell us that walking is good for us. It could also be good for Hogtown if its people could again walk the streets in safety and greet their neighbors along the way. The previous pictures of people walking and biking were all taken along the sidewalk in Madison Heights. Some of them were taken by Jimmie Ray, but others by unknown photographers. Several of the pictures of schoolchildren that appear in this book were taken by Jimmie in front of his home. The final three pictures in this chapter were taken of young people who lived in the neighborhood near H.M. Ray's store on Main Street.

The picture of the four children above was taken in front of H.M. Ray's store. They all lived within sight of the store. It was their neighborhood, a place where they knew everyone and everyone knew them. Even though I lived five blocks away in a different neighborhood I knew them too. I still recognized them when I saw this 60-plus year old picture. I only faltered at the first name of one of the girls and had to call Eugene for help. He remembered the picture, knew who was in it, and identified her over the telephone. Neither of us have phenomenal memories, but we do have some great memories. We remember the "good old days" and the special bond that exists between those of us who grew up together in Madison Heights.

The time is right for renewal of Hogtown. Solomon, the wisest man who ever lived, said, "Where there is no vision, the people perish" (Proverbs 29:18). May God give to this generation the necessary vision and commitment to renew our old hometown.

CHAPTER 33

The Madison Heights Goat

On one of my first picture-hunting expeditions for this book, Bill Layne loaned me a picture of "The Goat," or as it was often called in *The News and Advance*, "The Madison Heights Goat." For months, I have tried to decide how I could use the picture.

An adult nanny goat mysteriously appeared in Madison Heights in the late 1990s. She staked out her claim on the western slope of the bluff of Business 29 that leads north from The John Lynch Memorial Bridge. She immediately became a topic of conversation and a subject for pictures.

The Madison Heights goat

When several senior Madison Heights residents shared memories of their community in the *Amherst County Virginia Heritage Vol. II* (Walsworth Publishing Co. 2004). Charles Irvin, a lifetime resident, concluded his list with a "final two things." One of those things shocked me when he wrote: "We should not forget 'The Goat' that lived in peace on the hill for several years." With all due respect to my good friend Charles, I can imagine future generations going crazy trying to figure out what that statement means. Perhaps this article will help clarify it.

Charles Irvin said, "the goat lived in peace on the hill for several years." I'm not sure of the exact time of the goat's appearance, but I found one picture of it dated March 23, 1997. As far as I can determine, nobody knows where the goat came from. On April 1, 1999, *The News and Advance* reported the goat had been found dead two days earlier after "wandering the hill-side above the James River for at least half-dozen years." A year earlier the goat had been attacked by a trio of dogs—a pit bull, a lab and a chow—which were driven away with rocks by store employees and some customers from nearby 29 Market. When the same workers heard she was lying by the roadway dead, they closed their business and crossed the busy highway to see the goat. They were concerned that somebody may have shot it, but could not find any marks on her to determine the cause of her death. Some thought the dogs had killed her or run her into the path of an oncoming vehicle. Regardless, the goat was gone.

Will the goat become just a memory to the people of Madison Heights as Charles Irvin requested or will it become more? Will it become a representation of our community, a contemporary parable? Living in apparent peace and safety on the Amherst County bluff beside the James River, the goat was oblivious to the deadly danger that lurked nearby. One day it would take her life. Her days were numbered and she did not know it. If people who loved her had been aware of her plight they probably would have rushed to help, but now it is too late.

Today, the future existence of Madison Heights is being threatened by neglect, decay, apathy, and abandonment. Fortunately for Hogtown, there are those who are aware of the danger she is facing and are sounding the alarm to save her from destruction. The time to respond is now. If we wait, it will probably be too late.